Balaam's
Unofficial Handbook
of the United Church of Christ

Balaam's Unofficial Handbook

of the United Church of Christ

Balaam's Courier Staff

UNITED
CHURCH
PRESS®
Cleveland

*We gratefully dedicate this book to
Ron Buford,
who brought the comma, the Gracie Allen quote,
and the "God Is Still Speaking" campaign
to the United Church of Christ*

Contributors to this handbook include the following members of the *Balaam's Courier* staff:

Ted Braun	Tom Warren
Jan Bodin	Mark Lents, graphic artist

Balaam's Courier is an unofficial daily publication that has appeared at each UCC General Synod since 1975. It seeks to contribute challenging ideas and commentary from a biblical prophetic tradition, focusing on both our church's and our nation's life and mission.

United Church Press
700 Prospect Avenue
Cleveland, Ohio 44115-1100
unitedchurchpress.com

Scripture quotations unless otherwise noted are from the New Revised Standard Version Bible, copyright © 1989 by the Division of Christian Education of the National Council of the Churches of Christ in the U.S.A., and are used by permission.

Printed in the United States of America on acid-free paper that contains post-consumer fiber.

12 11 10   5 4

Library of Congress Cataloging-in-Publication Data

Balaam's unofficial handbook of the United Church of Christ / Balaam's Courier staff, Ted Braun, Jan Bodin, Tom Warren.
    p. cm.
    Includes index.
    ISBN 978-0-8298-1797-3 (alk. paper)
    1. United Church of Christ – Handbooks, manuals, etc. I. Braun, Ted. II. Bodin, Jan. III. Warren, Tom.
BX9885.B35 2008
285.8′34 – dc22   2008019527

An explanation of the symbols on the cover is given on pages 13–14.

Contents

About This Book

For new member classes and anyone who has ever sought to explain the United Church of Christ to family and friends, here is a resource to help you. Written with a light touch and a passion for the life and work of the UCC, this handbook provides historical, biblical, and theological insights into issues that have challenged the church throughout the ages.

In these pages you will find that the faith of the United Church of Christ is over two thousand years old. Yet our thinking is not. A denomination that has many "firsts" to its credit, the UCC seeks to speak God's extravagant welcome to everyone.

It was this denomination and its forebears that were the first to ordain a woman, an African American, and a gay man. It was this denomination and its forebears that began colleges and universities. It was this denomination that saw an urgent need for medical care and in response founded the Deaconess Society.

Taking the Bible seriously but not literally, our denomination strives to witness to the good news of Jesus Christ in thought and in action. We invite you to meet again the United Church of Christ.

Unofficial Handbook Guides

Greetings from Numbers 22! You know the story — the one about Balak the king of Moab, Balaam the prophet, and me, the prophet's donkey. You don't? Well, let me clue you in.

As God's people, the Israelites, are approaching Moab from Egypt, a fearful Balak summons Balaam to come and curse them, thinking that he can manipulate Balaam by offering him wealth and honor. Balaam reluctantly agrees to go on the condition that he not be forced to go against God's wishes.

On the way an angel suddenly appears on the road, seen only by — you guessed it — me! Well, I veer off the road and catch a beatin' from Balaam. But the angel comes back and this time, again trying to avoid the angel, I scrape Balaam's foot against a wall and am beaten again. Well, we all know that bad news comes in threes, so the angel comes back and, well, you get the picture. . . .

This time around though, I speak up. Enough is enough! In the midst of my complaining, Balaam's eyes are opened, and he too sees the angel. Balaam apologizes to the angel, confesses his sin, and is allowed to continue on his journey as long as he speaks only what God tells him.

Numbers 22 is a story about listening. Listening for what God is saying to the world. Listening for what God is saying to leaders and prophets and just plain old normal folks in the pews. And, most importantly, listening for what God is saying to the United Church of Christ. As you shall find out in this book, we UCCers believe that God has spoken to the world throughout history, that God is still speaking, and that we are called to listen — and to act!

Yet listening and acting are tricky endeavors. What are we to be listening for? On whose behalf are our actions? If on God's, how are we to know when God is speaking? If God's kingdom, how are we to know what God's kingdom looks like? To answer these difficult questions, let me introduce you to my good friend Evangeline, whom we meet in the book of Isaiah.

In Isaiah 11, you can read Isaiah's messianic vision. He describes a time when all violence will cease, a time when wild animals and domestic animals will be able to live together. Here are the words from verse 7:

> The cow and the bear shall graze,
> their young shall lie down together;
> and the lion shall eat straw like the ox.

The messianic age would be more than a time when odd pairings of animals would get along. It would be an age when people would be ruled by delight in God and righteousness would be the norm.

How does this vision feed our UCC spirits? If we believe that God is still speaking, how does God speak through this vision?

These were some of the questions that ambled through this old donkey's mind. So you can imagine my delight when it was discovered that on a dairy farm in western Wisconsin there was born a Holstein cow embodying Isaiah's vision and the hope of the UCC. That cow was found to have the courage to befriend a bear

that had wandered into her barn. Farmer Gutnuus, who knew a little Greek, named that bovine Evangeline, or "Good News." She was special, for one of her beautiful Holstein spots was exactly a comma. Evangeline was the other perfect spokes-creature for the unofficial UCC handbook.

P.S. Jim Moys, a reporter for the *American Questioner,* received a phone call one day from Tom Breitman. Tom was a neighbor of media-shy Farmer Gutnuus. Tom said, for a hundred dollars, he would give Moys the whole story and even sneak into Gutnuus's barn to get a few photos. Moys told Breitman it was a deal. When the story and the photos were ready to go to print, Moys completed a payment voucher for Breitman. Unfortunately, only the check request made it to the accounting department. The substantiating document never arrived through interoffice mail. The accountant called the reporter and sang, "Pardon me, Moys, is that the chap that knew the Gutnuus?"

Our Cover Story

What do the four symbols on the cover signify to you? They all have special meaning for the United Church of Christ. The first three — cross, crown, and orb — are part of the official UCC logo.

The **cross,** the main symbol of Christianity, reminds us of the life and death of Jesus. It was the main instrument of capital punishment for the Roman Empire in Jesus' day. Does it seem strange that his followers should have chosen this instrument of death as its chief symbol? It is a symbol that confronts us with many probing questions. Why did the Romans decide to put Jesus to death? What was there about Jesus that was considered such a subversive threat to the Roman Empire?

The **crown** symbolizes the sovereignty of Christ. It seems strange to connect a crown to an instrument of death, but this connection makes a bold statement that this victim of the Roman Empire, and not Caesar, is our Lord and Savior. In Christian tradition, this double symbol has been called a "Cross of Victory" or the "Cross Triumphant," reminding us of Jesus' resurrection and God's veto of the Roman verdict of death.

The **orb** (the circle with an equator) symbolizes the world. It reminds us of Jesus' command to his followers to be his "witnesses in Jerusalem and in all Judea and Samaria and to the ends of the earth" (Acts 1:8) — in all parts of the world claimed by Caesar's empire. We see this mandate as a calling to Christian witness and service, unity and ecumenical cooperation, in today's world. At the bottom of the logo are the words of Jesus' prayer "that they may all be one" (John 17:12).

The fourth symbol, the **comma,** seems at first to be a strange one to include with the others. It has become an important symbol for the UCC only recently. A crucial clue to unlocking its meaning comes from a quote by Gracie Allen,[1] "Never place a period where God has placed a comma. . . . " In the ongoing dialogue between God and human beings, there is never a final period but rather there is "yet more" to understand from the still-speaking God.

"God is still speaking" has become an important theological understanding in the UCC today. God's word creates worlds, humans, and shalom, and we humans struggle to hear it correctly, debating whether we hear periods or commas. In the UCC, we believe Jesus was a comma person. We invite you to read further about how followers of this comma person through the ages, and how the UCC in particular, have sought to be obedient to a still-speaking God.

---

1. Gracie Allen, a Christian, was a radio, film, and television personality with George Burns, her Jewish husband, during the mid-twentieth century.

Looking at Our UCC History

MEETING THE UNITED CHURCH OF CHRIST
AGAIN FOR THE FIRST TIME

Do you know the amazing story of the UCC? The United Church and the United States have intertwined in a remarkable way throughout their histories.

One strand of our forebears — the Pilgrims and Puritans — came to this New World from England in the 1600s to find freedom from an Anglican state church. As they departed the Old World, their pastor, John Robinson, urged them to keep their minds and hearts open to new ways: "God has yet more light and truth to break forth out of his holy Word." This recognition of a still-speaking God made a deep impression upon them and upon the generations that followed.

John Winthrop, one of the new arrivals at Plymouth, prayed that "we shall be as a city upon a hill...the eyes of all people are upon us." This vision of an exemplary community built on the principles of justice, peace, and faithful obedience also made a profound impression upon the new settlers.

Creating such a community, however, was harder than praying for it. The Congregationalists established a state church in Massachusetts. Dissidents were not easily suffered. The Baptist Roger Williams was banished to Rhode Island and Quaker Mary Dyer was hanged as a heretic on Boston Square.

Still, our forebears played important roles in the struggle for independence from England. In 1773 angry colonists in Boston gathered in the Meeting House of Old South to demand repeal of an unjust tax on tea. Their protest turned into the first act of civil disobedience in U.S. history: the "Boston Tea Party." Dressed as Indians, men boarded a ship in the harbor and threw the tea overboard. We are proud today that our forebears took this civil action, but regret their attempts to blame Native Americans for it.

Our Reformed Church predecessors who had come to Pennsylvania from Germany in the 1700s also played a part in the revolutionary struggle. In 1777, the British occupied Philadelphia, seat of the Continental Congress. It became known that they planned to melt down the Liberty Bell to manufacture cannons. The bell was covered with hay and transported to Zion Reformed Church in Allentown, where it was hidden under the floorboards.

Additionally, our forebears contributed to our country's educational development. They established colleges (Harvard, Yale, Wellesley, Smith, Dartmouth, Williams, Amherst, Oberlin, Mount Holyoke, Howard, Elmhurst, and others). They founded the first Protestant seminary in this country (Andover), the first school for the deaf community in the nation (the Connecticut Asylum for the Education of Deaf and Dumb Persons, later becoming Gallaudet University), and the first publishing house in the United States (The Pilgrim Press).

The contributions did not stop there. When our Evangelical Church predecessors came to the Midwest from Germany in the 1800s (after a union of Lutheran and Reformed traditions there), they established benevolent institutions such as deaconess hospitals, orphans' homes, and homes for the aged. They brought a pietistic fervor and an ecumenical bent. Their motto was "In essentials, unity; in non-essentials, diversity; in all things, charity [love]" (believed to come originally from St. Augustine).

During this history we have sought to be attentive to "comma faithfulness" and a still-speaking God: welcoming and benefiting from the gifts of African Americans, women, homosexual persons, and people with disabilities. In many cases, we encountered opposition from those quoting biblical verses citing discarded law codes and customs in support of slavery, segregation, patriarchalism, and exclusion. Instead, we have found our authority in the welcoming and integrating life and mission of Jesus, in perceiving and acting upon what he was passionate about: compassion, community, inclusion, love, forgiveness, healing, and sharing.

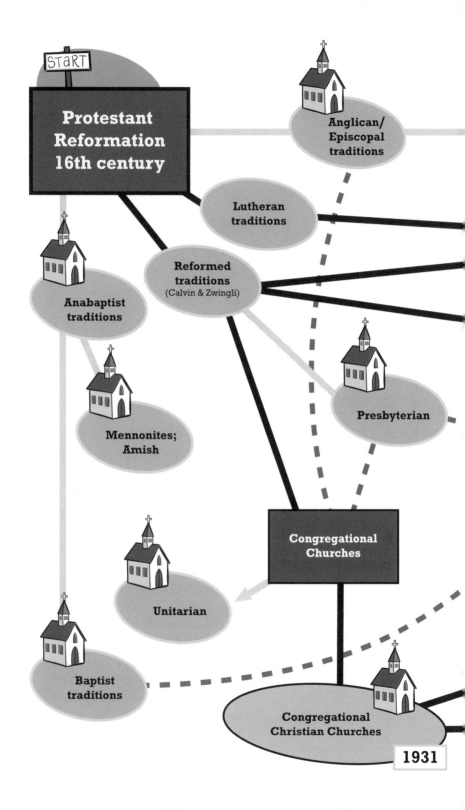

START

Protestant Reformation 16th century

Anglican/ Episcopal traditions

Lutheran traditions

Reformed traditions
(Calvin & Zwingli)

Anabaptist traditions

Mennonites; Amish

Presbyterian

Congregational Churches

Unitarian

Baptist traditions

Congregational Christian Churches

1931

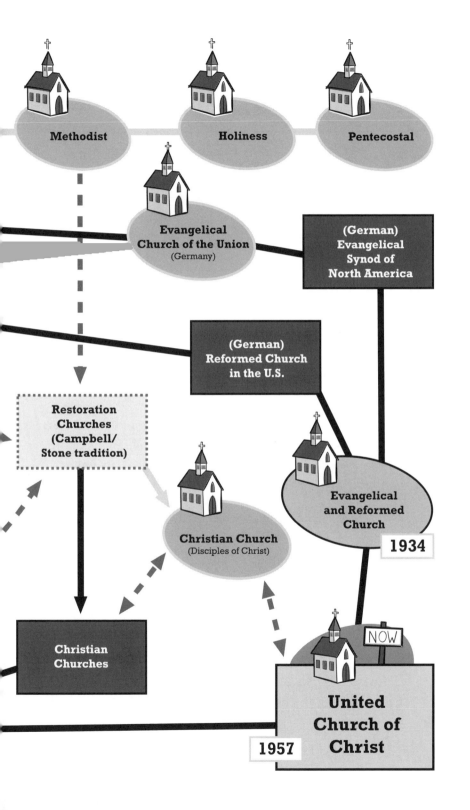

Methodist

Holiness

Pentecostal

Evangelical
Church of the Union
(Germany)

(German)
Evangelical
Synod of
North America

(German)
Reformed Church
in the U.S.

Restoration
Churches
(Campbell/
Stone tradition)

Christian Church
(Disciples of Christ)

Evangelical
and Reformed
Church

1934

Christian
Churches

NOW

United
Church of
Christ

1957

OUR HISTORICAL FAMILY ALBUM

Valuing the lives and gifts of African Americans in the life and mission of the church

+ In 1770 Samuel Sewall wrote the first anti-slavery pamphlet, *The Selling of Joseph,* in our country.

+ In 1773 Phillis Wheatley, a member of Old South Church in Boston, became the first published African American author.

+ In 1785 Lemuel Haynes became the first African American ordained by a Protestant denomination.

+ In 1839 Congregationalists in New England organized to support the African slaves who mutinied and took control of the schooner *Amistad,* ending up in a Connecticut jail. The court case revolved around the question of whether the slaves were still the property of the Spanish slave owner or whether they were free human beings. The Supreme Court ruled that the captives were not property, and the Africans regained their freedom.

+ In 1846 as a result of the *Amistad* case, the American Missionary Association — the first anti-slavery society in the United States with multi-racial leadership — was organized.

- In 1862 members of the First Congregational Church in Oberlin, Ohio, joined with members of Oberlin College and the local community to defy the Fugitive Slave Law and rescue a runaway slave, John Price.

- Between 1862 and 1877 the American Missionary Society founded six historically black colleges: Dillard, Fisk, LeMoyne-Owen, Huston-Tillotson, Talladega, and Tougaloo.

- In 1976 Joseph H. Evans was elected president of the UCC. He became the first African American leader of a racially integrated church in the United States.

Valuing the lives and gifts of women in the life and mission of the church

- Before 1818, women in the Christian Movement ("Christian female laborers") concluded that Paul never meant to prohibit women from praying aloud, singing, witnessing, exhorting, or preaching in public so long as men were permitted to carry out their governance roles in the fellowship.

- Women such as Nancy Gove Cram, Abigail Roberts, Rebecca Miller, and Ann Rexford all maintained vital ministries, but without ordination.

- In 1853, Antoinette Brown became the first woman in the United States to be ordained.

- In 1889, the Evangelical Deaconess Society and the Evangelical Home and Hospital were founded in St. Louis. Katherine Haack, a trained nurse and widow of an Evangelical pastor, was the first deaconess to be consecrated. Sixteen hospitals and institutions for health care and nurse training were consecrated.

Valuing the lives and gifts of lesbian, gay, bisexual, and transgender persons in the life and mission of the church

• In 1972 William R. Johnson became the first openly gay person to be ordained to a mainline Protestant ministry. The ordination of the first lesbian minister soon followed. In the following three decades, General Synod urged equal rights for homosexual citizens and called on congregations to welcome gay, lesbian, bisexual, and transgender members.

• In 2005 General Synod overwhelmingly passed a resolution supporting same-gender marriage equality — the first mainline denomination in the United States to do so. As UCC President John Thomas has said, "The General Synod of the United Church of Christ has acted courageously to declare freedom, affirming marriage equality, affirming the civil rights of same-gender couples to have their relationships recognized as marriages by the state, and encouraging our local churches to celebrate and bless those marriages."

Valuing the lives and gifts of persons with disabilities in the life and mission of the church

• In 1977 Harold H. Wilke, a UCC minister born without arms, was called to become the first executive of our UCC Disabilities Ministry. He was instrumental in the passage of the Americans with Disabilities Act.

BEYOND RACE, PATRIARCHY, AND PRIVILEGE

Just as God delivered the Israelite people from the cruel oppression of the Egyptians, God delivered us and is delivering us from cruel interpretations of scripture. Speaking through the diverse voices and experiences of the human family, God comes to be known as a God of justice, freedom, liberation, and love. The work of feminists, womanists, mujerista theologians, liberation theologians, Jewish historians and theologians, lesbian and gay commentators, and others have enriched the United Church of Christ and its understanding of the mission of the church and the role and authority of the Bible.

God's revelation appears in the work of feminist biblical scholars like Elisabeth Schüssler Fiorenza, who reminds us that a biblical word that does not liberate does not have authority. Her words are echoed by women's voices from around the world, including those from Africa, Latin America, and Asia.

Introducing the world to the vision of the Bible from the underside of history, these witnesses ask questions about the role of the Bible in perpetuating myths of women's inferiority. They look at issues of class and race, of sexual preference and ethnicity as they are interwoven in scriptures, and they call for unweaving to be done in the name of truth and liberation.

The voices of these womanist, mujerista, Native American, Asian, and feminist thinkers call us to examine structures of patriarchy that deny peoples their right to be empowered and free, to live with dignity and respect. They demand that the authority of the canon and of the scriptures be questioned in order that God may more clearly be heard.

Women and men from Latin America raise their many liberation voices reminding the Christian church that when anyone is oppressed, God's realm is fractured. They call the white church to step away from the head of the table and join in faith discussions with mutual respect and power.

Gay and lesbian persons witness to the church when they declare themselves to be called into ministry. They share with us the scriptural words and stories of hope that apply to them and to their lives of faith.

Jewish scholars, too, remind us that Judaism embraced a variety of expressions throughout history. Jews in the Diaspora record women as synagogue leaders and elders, suggesting that the

Christian witness is not simply an evolution of Jewish thought and practice, but a continuation of God's revelation throughout time.

The Christian church, therefore, is at its best when studying scripture, history, science, anthropology, and the arts in community with other believers: Christian, Jewish, Buddhist, Muslim, Hindu, and more. We are at our best when we learn from rich and poor, men and women, indigenous and not, formally educated and not.

God speaks many languages and is named many names. God touches the lives of people and calls them good. God calls us to embrace one another without prejudice or condescension and points the way to the beauty and truth of diversity.

SISTER SERVICE

In many ways, a deaconess was the counterpart to the Roman Catholic nun. She was consecrated in a service of worship. She adopted a particular garb that identified her as a religious woman. She was called Sister. She lived on a meager stipend and gave long hours of service, often as a nurse, but also as an assistant pastor, missionary, and teacher. She lived in community with other deaconesses.

In the deaconess tradition, however, she was free to leave her ministry if she chose to get married, or if she found she was no longer called to serve as she had been formerly. The deaconess movement in the history of the United Church of Christ can be traced to 1889 when the Evangelical Synod organized the first Deaconess Society. Approximately thirty years later, the Reformed Church began its deaconess work.

Through these ministries, hospitals and homes were established throughout the Midwest and beyond. They included Bensenville Home Society, Bensenville, Illinois; Caroline Mission, St. Louis, Missouri; Evangelical Children's Home, St. Louis, Missouri; Evangelical Home for the Aged, Rochester, New York; Good Samaritan

Home for the Aged, St. Louis, Missouri; St. Paul's Evangelical Old Folk's Home, Belleville, Illinois.

Deaconesses were trained in spiritual, intellectual, and social skills. Generally, they observed morning and evening prayers together. They provided a vital presence in the lives of the suffering sick and poor. They modeled lives of compassion and simplicity.

In the 1950s, the deaconess movement no longer sought recruits. Seminaries were opening their doors to women and to their callings in ministry. Ministry had changed.

Today we reflect on the history and contributions made by the deaconesses who served in our forebear denominations. Is there a place for persons who are called to live lives of such simplicity? Is there value to people intentionally choosing to live in community with one another? Is there an important witness that speaks truth to the power of consumerism? Is there a need for daily worship to keep us strong in the faith and mindful of our commitments?

It is said that monastic life grew strong when the Roman Empire permeated all of life. Those who took up monastic vows chose to embrace a life of service, witness, prayer, and obedience — not to empire but to God.

Today, monastic orders are beginning to grow again. Some Protestants are choosing to become oblates in Roman Catholic orders because there are no opportunities for them within their Protestant traditions. Other Protestants are seeking out spiritual directors to help them on their journeys of faith.

Perhaps we can ponder possibilities as we reflect on the great service of deaconesses, who like the Phoebe of Paul's writings, may be *diakonos* — sent as a messenger and helper.

T W O

Looking at Jesus

SPECIAL DELIVERY

Paul wrote several of the epistles, and yet Paul's writings, though very early in the history of the Christian church, mention nothing about Jesus' birth. In those first years of fledgling Christianity, people did not appear to be concerned about how and where Jesus was born. It probably was not until Jesus was of dating age that anyone really concerned themselves with his background — asking to meet his parents, what they did for work, whether or not they were devout believers, and how far they lived from the village waste management system.

When Matthew wrote his lineage story in his Gospel, he was careful to show how Jewish Jesus was, tracing Jesus' roots back in time from Abraham to Joseph, who was married to Mary, the mother of Jesus. Matthew's account is very simple. In a dream, Joseph was told that Mary was pregnant by the Holy Spirit and that he should marry her. Matthew reports that Joseph did just that. Then, after Jesus is born, there are wise men that come from the East, guided by a star.

In contrast, Luke begins his Gospel with the conception stories of John the Baptist and Jesus. As he reports the nativity story, he traces Jesus' family tree all the way back to Adam, emphasizing that Jesus was fully human. His account includes a report of a census, no vacancy at an inn, a manger, shepherds, and singing angels.

It should be said that nowhere in the scriptures is there a reference to a stable. The manger is mentioned, but the stable was a fanciful addition from religious artists around the fourteenth century. (Let it be known that the writers of this handbook have no desire to de-stable-ize the faith.)

It is also interesting to look closely at the first chapter of Matthew, where Jesus' genealogy is given. In verses 3, 5, and 6 four women's names appear. Tamar, Rahab, Ruth, and Bathsheba all had stories in the Bible. All offer challenging contrasts to a patriarchal society where women had little or no power. Tamar refuses to play her widow's role and seeks a partner in Judah (Gen. 38:14). Rahab, dwelling in her own home (a very unusual circumstance indeed), is a harlot (Josh. 2:2). Ruth is the woman who uncovers the feet (a euphemism for genitals) of Boaz at the threshing floor (Ruth 3:7). Bathsheba, whose husband, Uriah, is killed, comes to David (2 Sam. 11:4).

While it is easy to miss these references — for who really takes the time to read through the genealogies in the scriptures — they provide an important tension to the patriarchal system of old. In each case, these women exercised unusual non-patriarchal power. And, unlike stories of males in the scriptures, God did not intervene in their struggles. Their power, therefore, presents a creative tension in the shalom community of which Jesus was the leader. Women were not to be valued by their relationships to men. Rather they were regarded as people in their own right, children of God, beloved of God.

Finally, look at verse 16 in Matthew's first chapter. There Joseph is defined in terms of his relationship with Mary. He is simply called "the husband of Mary."

Matthew provides us then with a lengthy list of patriarchal connections (Abraham the father of Isaac, etc.) where women are not even important enough to mention, *and* a list of four women who challenge the patriarchal status quo.

If bringing these considerations to light raises other questions and reflections, then perhaps we *do* wish to destabilize the faith. At least a bit.

THE SHEPHERD FOR EWE

What words would you use to describe Jesus: peasant, teacher, faith healer, lawbreaker, troublemaker, reconciler, storyteller, subversive, liberator, rebel, blasphemer, heretic, savior, radical, redeemer, questioner of authority, Son of God, Lord?

All of these were different ways Jesus' contemporaries saw him — depending on whether they were poor peasants or rich people, supporters or antagonists, denigrated Samaritans or kosher Jews, colonial subjects or imperial colonizers. They — and all of us — have our particular lenses through which we view the world and other people.

Our picture of Jesus' life and mission comes primarily from the lenses of the first four books of the New Testament: Matthew, Mark, Luke, and John. They were written some forty or fifty years after Jesus' lifetime and present differing perspectives. As New Testament scholar John Dominic Crossan suggests, there is really only one Gospel in the Bible and four "according to's" because the life of Jesus has too much meaning to be limited to only one telling.

Mark emphasizes in stories the concerns of Jesus. Matthew portrays Jesus as a second Moses and emphasizes the kingdom of heaven. Luke emphasizes the poor and outcast and the plight of women. John emphasizes a Jesus of more formal discourses about water, bread, birth, lambs, light, and himself.

The four Gospels also begin their stories of Jesus at different starting points: Mark begins the Gospel story with Jesus' baptism, Matthew with his birth, Luke with his conception, and John with the beginning of God's spoken Word at the time of creation.

In these four Gospels we are reminded that Jesus was intimately acquainted with his Bible, especially the Teachings/Law (Torah) and the Prophets. He often quoted them. When he began his ministry in his hometown of Nazareth, he quoted verses from Isaiah to introduce the mandate for his ministry:

> The Spirit of the Lord is upon me, because he has anointed me to bring good news to the poor. He has sent me to proclaim release to the captives and recovery of sight to the blind, to let the oppressed go free, to proclaim the year of the Lord's favor. (Luke 4:18–19, from Isaiah 61:1, 58:6, 61:2a)

According to Luke, when Jesus was about to begin his ministry and was fasting in the wilderness in preparation, he was tempted by the devil to adopt self-serving methods and goals in his ministry (Luke 4:1–13). He rejected these temptations by quoting scripture:

> One does not live by bread alone. (Deut. 6:12)

> Worship the Lord your God, and serve only him. (Deut. 6:13)

> Do not put the Lord your God to the test. (Deut. 6:16)

What is more, in the Gospels of Matthew, Mark, and Luke, Jesus identifies the most important commandment as loving God with all your heart, soul, strength, and mind, and loving your neighbor as yourself (Matt. 22:39, Mark 12:21, Luke 10:27). "Love" for Jesus meant practicing compassion, kindness, mercy, and respect. "Neighbor" for Jesus included even foreigners, outcasts, and enemies (Matt. 5:43–44).

In his life and ministry, Jesus taught and modeled the nourishing, life-giving, all-embracing practice of compassion.

JESUS AND HIS COMMA DENOMINATOR

Jesus proclaimed a compassionate God who was constantly placing commas where others had placed periods. If laws, rules, or customs got in the way of acting with compassion, then people were to question and even disregard authority. As a person proclaiming a comma-placing God,

Jesus welcomed and included...

+ Foreigners (referred to in Jesus' first sermon in Nazareth). (Luke 4:16–30)
+ Samaritans (outcasts, second-class). (John 4:7–9; Luke 10: 29–37.
+ Women (as disciples, Luke 8:1–3), Samaritan woman at the well. (John 4:3–30)
+ Those isolated by physical or mental disability (blind, deaf, lame, paralyzed, suffering from skin disease, possessed by unclean spirits). (Matt. 11:1–5; Luke 7:22)

Jesus broke "purity" laws

+ Welcoming and eating with sinners. (Luke 15:1–2)
+ Not observing the ritual of washing before eating. (Mark 7:1–9, Luke 11:37)
+ Healing and eating grain on the Sabbath. (Luke 13:10–17; 13:14; 14:1–6; John 5:1–18)

Jesus urged his followers to observe a new ethic

+ You have heard that it was said, "An eye for an eye and a tooth for a tooth, but I say to you...." (Matt. 5:38–42)
+ You have heard that it was said, "You shall love your neighbor and hate your enemy, but I say to you...." (Matt. 5:43–48)

Jesus sought to establish a community based on sharing in opposition to the Roman type of community based on greed and exploitation

- Feeding of the four thousand/five thousand. (Matt. 15:32–38, Mark 6:30–44, Luke 9:10–17)
- Conversion of Zacchaeus to economic justice ("salvation"). (Luke 19:1–10)

Before Jesus came into his life, Zacchaeus, a little man, served the Roman Empire as a tax collector — which took quite a toll on his neighbors.

Jesus' passion for justice and solidarity with the poor and oppressed was threatening to the Roman Empire and its Jewish collaborators in Jerusalem. He was constantly placing a comma where the authorities had placed a period. He invited people to join God's kingdom (realm/empire) — one based on a different social, economic, and political value system than the Jewish-Roman one. As a result, he was followed around by representatives of the Jerusalem Temple, who dogged Jesus like truth squads, hoping to build a case against him and his alternative realm of God (Matt. 15:1–2). Still he set his face toward Jerusalem and the story continued.

JESUS WON, ROMANS NOTHING

When Jesus finally showed up in Jerusalem, he planned and carried out two prophetic protest demonstrations against the Jewish-Roman powers. The first was the counter-procession into Jerusalem, which we remember on Palm Sunday. Jesus processed into the city in humility on a donkey while, on the same day,

Pontius Pilate and his forces marched into Jerusalem with a great show of military might.[1]

Jesus' second prophetic protest took place the next day. Overturning the tables in the Temple (Mark 11:15). Jesus performed an act of civil disobedience against the Temple establishment (the center of the Jewish-Roman collaboration). Shortly thereafter he was crucified on a cross, the punishment for those who threatened the "peace" and order of the empire.

That should have been the end of the story. The Roman Empire had placed a final period to bring that story and life to a close. But something remarkable happened. Jesus' followers encountered a risen presence in their midst. This good news of the resurrection, like the good news accounts of Jesus in the Gospel stories, had much meaning for his followers. And so we have stories of Jesus greeting Mary and the other women on Easter morn, passing through a door to join his disciples in an upper room, joining the disciples for breakfast on the shore, walking beside a couple on the road to Emmaus, and coming in a voice to Paul along the Damascus Road.

It was another comma! There were still more to come!

---

1. See Marcus J. Borg and John Dominic Crossan, *The Last Week: A Day-by-Day Account of Jesus's Final Week in Jerusalem* (HarperSanFrancisco, 2006), 2–5.

JESUS AND THE TRINITY

The relationship between Jesus and God has been debated by the church down through the ages. Tertullian, an early church theologian in the second century, was the first to use the word "Trinity" to describe God. He maintained that there were three "persons" — Father, Son, and Holy Spirit — sharing one substance of Godness. Other church fathers argued that the word *persona* that Tertullian took to be "person" really meant "role" — the three roles played by the one God.

This resulted in great theological battles about how the three related to each other. Were the three in a hierarchical or a communitarian relationship to each other? Or was giving emphasis to "three" rather than to "one" the wrong road? Was the full humanity of Jesus being devalued? Was Jesus called "divine" mainly to counteract the divinity ascribed to Caesar? In the midst of all this contention about the *person* of Christ, there was little doubt about the central understanding of the *work* of Christ: "In Christ God was reconciling the world to himself" (2 Cor. 5:19).

In the early history of our Congregational forebears in New England this same controversy resulted in a division between Trinitarians and Unitarians. One approach was to use the word "Triune" instead of "Trinitarian" to describe God, the main emphasis being on the oneness or unity of God rather than on a word that suggested three divinities.

Two hymns side-by-side in *The New Century Hymnal* illustrate this dual heritage. "Holy, Holy, Holy" (#277, written in 1826) speaks of "God in three persons, blessed Trinity!" The next hymn, "Creator God, Creating Still" (#278, written in 1977 and revised in 1993) speaks of three functions rather than persons of God:

> "Creator God, creating still..."
> "Redeemer God, redeeming still..."
> "Sustainer God, sustaining still..."
> "Great Triune God..."

The author of the second hymn, Jane Parker Huber, commented that by describing the Triune God in terms of function, she hoped to avoid a tendency to think we know God by knowing formulas. This second hymn is an excellent one, too, for helping us envision a still-speaking, still-acting God — a God of commas rather than periods and final formulas.

Another helpful way to approach a threefold understanding of God is through human experience. We encounter God in three primary ways: God beyond us, God among us (most fully in Jesus), and God within us.

As Tom Harpur has written,

> God is above and around and within every one of us. . . . We believe God sent Jesus, anointing him in the power of Spirit, to declare by word and deed the gospel of personal and social liberation from the power of fear and all injustice and oppression. Though he was cruelly and unjustly murdered, God raised him from death and God's seal is set forever on Jesus' message and ministry. In him we know that God is love and that forgiveness and acceptance are ours always. In him we are called to realize God's kingdom in our own lives and in the lives of others. In him we are called to join with God in making all things new.[2]

Anne Squire addresses the subject of Jesus' "radical inclusion" even more directly:

> How well is this vision of radical inclusion being practiced in the world today? In our communities there is evidence of unjust social and economic relationships, oppressive political leadership, biased relationships, and as Walter Wink reminds us, "violence to maintain them all." Even in the church, which should be the very place where inclusion is

---

2. Tom Harpur, "New Creeds," in *The Emerging Christian Way: Thoughts, Stories, and Wisdom for a Faith of Transformation*, ed. Michael Schwartzentruber (Kelowna, B.C.: CopperHouse, 2006).

best practiced, we discover, in different degrees in different communities, restrictions on the sacraments, exclusion
of women from ordination, refusal to ordain or marry gays
and lesbians; and barriers to the poor, the disabled, and the
mentally challenged.[3]

This threefold encounter with a radical still-speaking God is
the main thrust of our UCC *Statement of Faith.* It places Jesus at
the center of this God-encounter for us. Unlike the Apostles' and
Nicene Creeds it does not jump from Jesus' birth to his death and
resurrection but fills in the gap with an affirmation concerning
the core of Jesus' mission on earth — and of our mission through
the church.

This Statement of Faith is as follows:

United Church of Christ
STATEMENT OF FAITH
(in the Form of a Doxology)

We believe in you, O God, Eternal Spirit,
God of our Savior Jesus Christ and our God,
   and to your deeds we testify:
You call the worlds into being,
   create persons in your own image,
   and set before each one the ways of life and death.
You seek in holy love to save all people from aimlessness
   and sin.
You judge people and nations by your righteous will
   declared through prophets and apostles.

In Jesus Christ, the man of Nazareth, our crucified and risen
   Savior,

---

3. Anne Squire, "Radical Inclusion," in *The Emerging Christian Way: Thoughts, Stories, and Wisdom for a Faith of Transformation,* ed. Michael Schwartzentruber (Kelowna, B.C.: CopperHouse, 2006).

you have come to us
and shared our common lot,
conquering sin and death
and reconciling the world to yourself.

You bestow upon us your Holy Spirit,
    creating and renewing the church of Jesus Christ,
    binding in covenant faithful people of
    all ages, tongues, and races.

You call us into your church
    to accept the cost and joy of discipleship,
    to be your servants in the service of others,
    to proclaim the gospel to all the world
    and resist the powers of evil,
    to share in Christ's baptism and eat at his table,
    to join him in his passion and victory.

You promise to all who trust you
    forgiveness of sins and fullness of grace,
    courage in the struggle for justice and peace,
    your presence in trial and rejoicing,
    and eternal life in your realm which has no end.

Blessing and honor, glory and power be unto you. Amen.

THREE

Looking at the Bible

THE BOOK SPEAKS VOLUMES

The spoken word has always had a central and powerful role in the biblical story. The creation narrative in Genesis begins by declaring, "In the beginning...God said...." A voice addresses Moses out of a burning bush and commissions him to bring an enslaved people out of Egypt. God speaks through the words of the prophets questioning and condemning authority that has been corrupted and behavior that has become unfaithful. Words throughout the Old Testament gather to form poems, songs, myths, histories, proverbs, laws, commandments, and liturgies.

Later, in the New Testament times, John opens his Gospel narrative with the same beginning as Genesis, "In the beginning was the Word," only now he uses the Greek word *logos* instead of the Hebrew *dabar.* But he uses it in an astonishing new context. This speaking of God, this word of God, has now become incarnate in Jesus' life and ministry. In the rest of the New Testament words are gathered in histories, letters, sermons, teachings, healings, blessings, and revelations, but always in relation now to a Word embodied and lived out in the life of the church.

At the core of Jesus' teachings are the words of his Beatitudes, which are part of his Sermon on the Mount (Matt. 5:3–12 and Luke 6:20–23). As William Sloane Coffin, a UCC pastor and author, has written, "The Beatitudes challenge today's habitual expectations. They shake up our usual criteria of normalcy by presenting a new view of reality. While sounding peaceful enough they are at heart profound and passionate, full of insights and authority for those of us prepared, in these perilous times, to reevaluate matters at the very core of our individual and collective lives."[1] And Marian Wright Edelman, a UCC member and president of the Children's Defense Fund, has commented on "the truly radical message the Beatitudes still carry for all of us — eight simple statements with the power to turn the world upside down."[2]

Beyond the core of Jesus' teachings, we must consider the whole Bible. It makes no claim to being the Word of God. Although the writer of 2 Timothy writes in 3:16 that "all scripture [referring to his Bible, the Old Testament] is inspired by God and is useful for teaching, for reproof, for correction, and for training in righteousness," we today find parts of the Old and New Testaments not particularly inspired or inspiring. There has been, however, an ongoing process of interpretation and reinterpretation within the span of the Bible and continuing up to the present time as new occasions imbued by a still-speaking God have brought new insights and truths.

---

1. William Sloane Coffin, in his foreword to Erik Kolbell, *What Jesus Meant: The Beatitudes and a Meaningful Life* (Louisville: Westminster John Knox Press, 2003), 10.

2. Marian Wright Edelman, in a comment on the back cover of Kolbell, *What Jesus Meant.*

The United Church of Christ recognizes this basic perspective. Our primary authority is not a created object, a book, but the Creator, the still-speaking God. And the primacy of this authority includes Jesus, the person through whom this God spoke and lived so passionately in our midst. The radically welcoming and inclusive teaching and practice of Jesus is our special authority.

And so this Bible has become the family album of our faith family. As we become increasingly familiar with it through rereading and study, there are several critical conditions that contribute to a greater understanding of God's word in the Bible and in our lives today.

Whenever one studies scripture, one should always come with a few basic questions: Who wrote this? Why? Whom was it written for? Is it descriptive or prescriptive? Are there other passages in scripture that dialogue with this passage? What form is it written in? How has this passage been interpreted by scholars throughout the ages? Is there anything missing? Without asking such questions, one may never go below the surface of understanding a text.

In the story of the feeding of the five thousand, for instance, women were not counted in that number. The story says almost as a footnote, "as well as women and children." If one asks, "Is there anything missing" when reading this text, one might come to the conclusion that the importance of women was missing!

In addition to the questions mentioned above, one should always study the Bible with an interpretive commentary or two. It helps to imagine these commentaries as leading you into a dark forest by the light of their lanterns. One does not necessarily know one's destination, but the light is important for the journey.

It is important as well to study the scriptures with other people. It is in the company of others that one is often given important insight. This is particularly true when a diversity of persons is present. What does a text mean to someone of means, to the poor, to people of color, to sexual minorities? It is in the community of others that we are most often able to find the challenges to grow our faith.

Finally, it is essential that we read and study the Bible with an eye for both historical context and present-day challenges. How did a text speak to the people hundreds and even thousands of years ago? How does it address what is happening today? In other words, God is still speaking. We need to be listening.

CHOSEN, NOT FROZEN

The authority of the Bible

The Bible is an invaluable resource book for us today because it is our *family* album. It gives us snapshots of our spiritual ancestors and tells about their struggle to hear and respond to a God speaking to them in their particular time and context.

The Bible's basic narrative

In the Old Testament, our family album describes how a God of justice brought our ancestors out of slavery and oppression in Egypt, making a covenant with them and challenging them to create a new kind of society based on justice, compassion, and faithfulness.

In the New Testament, our family album describes how in the time of the Roman Empire, God through Jesus continued this challenge, welcoming oppressed people — women, outcasts, the poor, people of all kinds — as well as those doing the oppressing into a new kind of society again based on justice, compassion, and faithfulness. Living this way was to experience shalom — peace, wholeness, and salvation.

The Bible's historical conditioning

Our family album, the container for this basic narrative, raises a number of interesting problems for us, however. It was produced in a time when humans did not have as much information as we have today about the formation of the various worlds we live in — the universe, our planet, our bodies, and our inner worlds. Human societies, both in Old Testament and New Testament times, were profoundly hierarchical and patriarchal. Kings, pharaohs, emperors, high priests, rich landowners, fathers, husbands, men were on top in the social, economic, political, and family structures. Women, children, and slaves were underneath them in the ordering.

As Old Testament scholar Walter Brueggemann has commented, "The Bible is marked by, indeed saturated by ideology, ... an assertion of truth that contains covert dimensions of vested interest." This partisan advocacy "includes ethnicity that tilts toward racism and patriarchalism that endlessly casts women in subservient roles. The partly hidden commitments of ethnocentrism and patriarchalism move in the direction of violence in a variety of forms."[3]

Biblical authority is chosen

The authority of the Bible is not inherent in the text or forced on us but is chosen by individuals or by a group of people to have authority for us. We confer it.

---

3. Walter Brueggemann, *An Introduction to the Old Testament: The Canon and Christian Imagination* (Nashville: Abingdon Press, 1993.

People have gone to the Bible and found support for endorsing slavery, devaluing women, demonizing homosexuals, killing enemies, and revering even the most corrupt and evil governments. They have used its "authority" to exclude and punish people. This happens when we claim that a text written thousands of years ago in the context of a different worldview transcends history and trumps human knowledge and experience today. This happens when various historically conditioned verses are "cherry-picked" and the basic narrative is ignored.

We can make an important distinction at this point. What happened in the biblical past may be *descriptive* of that time for us, but not *prescriptive* for us in our time. As James Russell Lowell wrote in his poem "Once to Every Man and Nation":

> New occasions teach new duties,
> Time makes ancient good uncouth;
> They must upward still and onward,
> Who would keep abreast of truth.

What is especially interesting is that there is a continual "traditioning" process going on both within the Bible and since its completion. Because we are always dealing with a still-speaking

God, no account of traditioning can ever turn out to be a "final" one. As Brueggemann reminds us, it is always open to newer versions that rearticulate our faith in the intellectual categories and cultural environments of new contexts. Jesus and Paul were doing this kind of rearticulating throughout their ministries.

Our biblical authority today

Down through the years, people reading our family album have been inspired to struggle for justice and peace, practice nonviolence, respond to hatred with love and forgiveness, and extend an extravagant welcome to outcasts and those stigmatized by contemporary purity codes.

Thankfully, we have the example of Jesus, who ignored the walls that deprive us of community. He leads us out of the boxes that limit our compassion and into an extravagant welcome that invites both the stranger and God into our lives. God has also given us new understandings about being human, managing our planet, defining our common good, and being God's people in the world.

We need to be very careful that the Bible does not become an icon, boxing God in. Our primary authority is not a created object, a book, but the Creator, the still-speaking God. And the primacy of this authority was exemplified by Jesus, the person through whom this God spoke and lived so passionately in our midst. The radically welcoming and inclusive teaching and practice of Jesus is our special authority.

UNDERSTANDING "VERSES" UNDERSTANDING

Biblical Weaponry 101

In past years churches (especially those controlled by white males) have used biblical verses as weapons against people of color and women. They have used these verses to justify slavery and segregation and to keep women in submissive roles. Fortunately, most churches today have moved past that.

Today, however, a number of congregations are using biblical verses as weapons against those who have a homosexual or
bisexual orientation. They claim that, according to the Bible,
homosexuality is a sin and that congregations and denominations
should not be affirming this kind of "lifestyle." This is causing division in many denominations and prompting some congregations
to secede from their denominational membership. Indeed, this is
one of the main theological issues challenging the church today.

This is not as serious a problem in the United Church of Christ
as in some denominations because of its strong emphasis on God's
extravagant welcoming and on Jesus' passionate inclusiveness. Because of the UCC's historic emphasis on education and Bible
study, it is important to take a look at several of these weapons,
analyze their context, and show how new understanding can help
disarm them.

Following are four of the main biblical weapons being used
against lesbian, gay, bisexual, and transgender people today. (All
examples are from the New Revised Standard Version except for

one, so indicated, from the New King James Version.) Following these verses you will find important contextual information.

1. "You shall not lie with a male as with a woman; it is an abomination" (Lev. 18:22). "If a man lies with a male as he lies with a woman, both of them have committed an abomination; they shall be put to death" (Lev. 20:13).

2. "Claiming to be wise, they became fools; and they exchanged the glory of the immortal God for images resembling a mortal human being or birds or four-footed animals or reptiles. Therefore God gave them up in the lusts of their hearts to impurity, to the degrading of their bodies among themselves, because they exchanged the truth about God for a lie and worshiped and served the creature rather than the Creator, who is blessed forever! Amen.

   "For this reason God gave them up to degrading passions. Their women exchanged the natural intercourse for unnatural, and in the same way also the men, giving up natural intercourse with women, were consumed with passion for one another. Men committed shameless acts with men and received in their own persons the due penalty of their error. And since they did not see fit to acknowledge God, God gave them up to a debased mind and to things that should not be done. They were filled with every kind of wickedness, evil, covetousness, malice. Full of envy, murder, strife, deceit, craftiness, they are gossips, slanderers, God-haters, insolent, haughty, boastful, inventors of evil, rebellious toward parents, foolish, faithless, heartless, ruthless" (Rom. 1:22–32).

3. "Do you not know that wrongdoers will not inherit the kingdom of God? Do not be deceived! Fornicators, idolaters, adulterers, male prostitutes, sodomites, thieves, the greedy, drunkards, revilers, robbers — none of these will inherit the kingdom of God" (1 Cor. 6:9–10).

"Do you not know that the unrighteous will not inherit the kingdom of God? Do not be deceived. Neither fornicators, nor idolaters, nor adulterers, nor homosexuals, nor sodomites, nor thieves, nor covetous, nor drunkards, nor revilers, nor extortioners will inherit the kingdom of God" (1 Cor. 6:9–10, NKJV).

4. "We know that the law is good, if one uses it legitimately. This means understanding that the law is laid down not for the innocent but for the lawless and disobedient, for the godless and sinful, for the unholy and profane, for those who kill their father or mother, for murderers, fornicators, sodomites, slave traders, liars, perjurers, and whatever else is contrary to the sound teaching that conforms to the glorious gospel of the blessed God, which he entrusted to me" (1 Tim. 1:8–11).

A WEAPON DISARMAMENT PROCESS

The context of the Leviticus passages

These two verses refer to the practice of cult prostitution in ancient Israel. A clue to this context is given in Deuteronomy 23:17: "None of the daughters of Israel shall be a temple prostitute; none of the sons of Israel shall be a temple prostitute."

These two verses (which do not include any prohibition against lesbian sexual experience) are part of Israel's holiness code of ritual purity. This code also prohibited eating meat with blood in it, intercourse during a menstrual period, crossbreeding animals, sowing two kinds of seed in the same field, wearing garments of mixed fabrics, and working on the Sabbath.

The word "abomination" (*toevah*) referred to sacral contamination — ritual uncleanness or religious idolatry. Selecting just two verses out of this long list of ancient purity codes in order to condemn people today because of their sexual orientation (while conveniently overlooking all the other prohibitions) is a highly questionable practice. Health professionals today recognize that homosexual orientation is as natural for some people as heterosexual orientation is for others. Similarly, left-handedness is natural for a minority of people.

The context of the Romans verses

Near the end of his third missionary journey through Asia Minor and Greece, Paul in Corinth wrote a letter to the young church in Rome, which he had not yet visited. All along his journey he had encountered great temples built to honor Aphrodite, Diana, and other fertility gods and goddesses, all of these featuring temple prostitutes and sexual depravity. Paul saw the worshipers at these temples as worshiping the creature rather than the Creator. In his letter Paul talked about humanity's sinfulness (we are all sinners who have fallen short of the glory of God) and how salvation and wholeness is offered by God through Christ as a free gift of grace. To select a few verses out of this letter to condemn present-day Christians for their homosexual orientation is a gross injustice.

Paul also discusses how natural a man and woman's relationship is for intercourse and for producing children. This is not to imply, however, that relationships that do not lead to producing children cannot be natural, as well. Some couples are unable to have children; some choose not to have children; some are too old to have children; some choose to adopt children; and some people remain single. A homosexual orientation for some is natural. Paul was not addressing such an orientation in this passage.

The context of the Corinthian verses

In his letter to the Corinthian church, Paul mentions ten categories of "wrongdoers" or "unjust ones" (*adikoi*):

1. *pornoi:* prostitutes, fornicators

2. *eidololatrai:* idolaters

3. *mochai:* adulterers

4. *malakoi:* soft young call boys (translated as "male prostitutes" in the NRSV, "homosexuals" in the NKJV, "sexual pervert" in the Revised English Bible, "boy prostitutes" in the New American Bible, "the self-indulgent" in the New English Bible)[4]

5. *arsenokoitai:* pederasts, adult customers hiring "soft" young call boys (translated in the NRSV as "sodomites")[5]

6. *kleptai:* thieves

7. *pleonektai:* covetous, avaricious, or greedy persons

8. *methusoi:* drunkards

9. *loidoroi:* revilers, railers

10. *harpages:* robbers, extortioners, rapacious persons

The context of the Timothy verses

The writer of the first letter to Timothy lists five categories of sins:

1. Legal behavior: lawless and disobedient.

2. Religious behavior: godless and sinful, unholy and profane.

3. Violent behavior: patricide, matricide, murder.

---

4. It is obvious that the translators had a difficult time agreeing on the meaning of the Greek word *malakoi.* The NKJV translators, however, made a mistake by using the contemporary term "homosexuals." What Paul is condemning here is not homosexuality per se, but unloving, victimizing, idolatrous sexuality. Again, to apply this list to present-day Christians of homosexual orientation is a gross injustice.

5. It is unfortunate that the NRSV translators chose the word "sodomites" to convey the meaning of *arsenokoitai.* According to Ezekiel's definition, sodomites were haughty people who "had pride, excess of food, and prosperous ease, but did not aid the poor and needy" (Ezek. 16:49–50). One can point to many such sodomites in our U.S. society and government!

Another question for Bible-readers today: Should we be more concerned about the last five categories in Paul's list: thieves, greedy persons, drunkards, revilers, extortioners? What about greedy CEOs who get astronomical incomes and golden parachute bonuses when they leave their jobs? Greedy nations that covet other nations' resources? Citizens who covet huge McMansions? People who have plenty and want more, while so many around the world do not have enough to live.

4. Social/sexual behavior:

> *pornois:* prostitutes, fornicators.

> *arsenokoitais:* pederasts, adult customers hiring young call boys (translated in the NRSV as "sodomites," see note above).

> *andrapodistais:* slave traders, kidnappers (of little boys for sexual use), pimps.

5. Moral behavior (trustworthiness): liars, perjurers.

Once again, the Bible has nothing in it to condemn homosexual orientation as we understand it. Its litmus test for everyone is loving God with all one's heart, soul, mind, and strength, and one's neighbor as oneself. Every human being is a precious child of God, a temple for God's spirit. And every relationship is blessed when it affirms and enhances our humanity.

REMOVE THE DECALOGUE
FROM YOUR OWN EYE

The Ten Commandments have become one of the most popular icons in our country. We find them displayed in public places such as schools, senior citizen centers, courthouses, churches, and front yards. One Alabama judge even installed a two-ton stone monument of the commandments in his state courthouse, but was later forced to remove it. He then took the monument on a "veneration trip" around the country so that people could see and touch it.

Why have these commandments become such a potent symbol for us today, especially since only three of the prohibited activities — murder, theft, and perjury — have any judicial standing as crimes? In contrast, some of the other prohibitions — idolatry, adultery, coveting, and forgetting to keep the Sabbath holy — seem to be widely ignored.

It is important for those who believe that God is still speaking in moral imperatives today to "unpack" the Decalogue. Two versions of the Ten Commandments (actually "Words" or "Statements" in the original Hebrew) are found in the Bible: in Exodus 20:2–17 and Deuteronomy 5:6–21.

First, it is important to recognize their patriarchal context as a time-bound one. Most of our public Decalogues use a shortened generic version to get away from the patriarchal bias in the original text. For example, the last commandment states "You shall not covet your neighbor's house; you shall not covet your neighbor's wife." It does not mention anything, however, about not coveting your neighbor's husband! This is because women at that time were considered to be the property of their husbands (or their fathers). Many of our contemporary Decalogue signs solve that problem by stating only "Do not covet." But this gets us into an even greater problem since coveting is at the core of our consumerist, advertising world.

Secondly, it is also important to recognize that there are differences in the Jewish, Protestant, and Catholic versions of the Decalogue. These differences depend on how the Hebrew words have been translated, how the commandments have been numbered, and, most importantly, whether God's introduction to the commandments (which establishes their basic religious context) is included in these contemporary listings. Interestingly, this crucial religious rationale is provided only in the Jewish version.

God's full introduction to the Decalogue states, "I am the Lord your God, who brought you out of the land of Egypt, out of the house of slavery." This context is crucial for the Ten Commandments: they are addressed to a covenant community formed out of God's passion for human liberation, and they point to a new social possibility for this community — an alternative society to be organized on principles of justice and peace in a new land of promise. They call for obedience and loyalty to this God of liberation who will guide the covenant community in reshaping its human relations in healing and liberating ways.

Contemporary Decalogue signs generally omit the phrase "who brought you out of the land of Egypt, out of the house of slavery." After the phrase "I am the Lord your God" they place a period instead of a comma, thereby ignoring the crucial historical encounter and context for this declaration.

In similar fashion, the signs omit the religious rationale for keeping the Sabbath holy. In the Exodus 20:1–17 account, it is because God rested on the seventh day of creation. In the Deuteronomy 5:6–21 account, it is because God had delivered the Jews from slavery in Egypt, and a new economic order was being inaugurated. Everyone was to be given a weekly day of rest from work and production!

Placing a Decalogue sign in a front yard or on a wall should commit the sign-placers to participation in an ongoing theological dialogue about a radical God who calls us to participate in a radically new relationship and agenda. For example:

The first four commandments focus on our relations to God. They speak of a God who has now displaced every other loyalty, who cannot be harnessed into our own interests and ideology. God's name is not to be used in the service of some purpose that is foreign to God's character and mission (such as using God's name to legitimize our nation's wars or to bless an individual's pursuit of political office). In an environment of endless productivity, frantic consumption and consumerism, and worker exploitation, this God calls us to practice Sabbath rest and disengagement.

The last six commandments focus on neighbor relations: honoring parents and family relationships of fidelity, and creating a society not corrupted by murder, theft, false witness, or coveting. This is a challenge for us today when we live in the midst of an economic order based on coveting. Ironically, in the midst of this economic order we live in a world where people's selfhood is stolen because they do not have the necessary goods or support to make a life of dignity possible. We have a government that goes to war based on lies, false witness, and secrecy. These are the kinds of issues that the posting of the Ten Commandments all across our country should be prompting.

To promote the commandments without including this dynamic, God-filled context is to try to build a society on sterile legalisms without being addressed by a still-speaking God. Perhaps there are new commandments that we should be listening to today to lead us in new directions. As Katha Pollitt has written, "How different history would have been had [God] clearly and unmistakably forbidden war, tyranny, taking over other people's countries, slavery, exploitation of workers, cruelty to children, wife-beating, stoning, treating women — or anyone — as chattel or inferior beings."[6] This all depends, however, on what kind of authority we grant to such commandments.

Will you find a copy of the Ten Commandments on the walls of most UCC churches? Probably not, although a shortened version is included in the General Resources section of the UCC *Book of Worship*. Several definitions of the word "icon" in *Webster's Dictionary* suggest reasons for this: "a conventional religious image," "an object of uncritical devotion," "an idol."

In our struggle to listen to a God who is constantly using commas rather than periods, we have discovered surprising new truths. This still-speaking God calls all of us into unconventional imaging and imagining, into a loyal devotion that is critical of all the idolatries that tempt us today — a covenantal relationship that

---

6. Katha Pollitt, "Stacked Decalogue," *The Nation*, September 22, 2003.

goes far beyond the words of a shortened, ahistorical Decalogue on some wall or in someone's yard.

NOT JUST IDOL TALK:
THE TEN COMMANDMENTS

1. I am the Lord your God. You shall have no other gods before me.

2. You shall not make for yourself an idol, whether in the form of anything that is in heaven above, or that is on the earth beneath, or that is in the water under the earth.

3. You shall not make wrongful use of the name of the Lord your God for the Lord will not acquit anyone who misuses his name.

4. Remember the Sabbath day, and keep it holy.

5. Honor your father and your mother.

6. You shall not murder.

7. You shall not commit adultery.

8. You shall not steal.

9. You shall not bear false witness against your neighbor.

10. You shall not covet your neighbor's house; you shall not covet your neighbor's wife, or male or female slave, or ox, or donkey, or anything that belongs to your neighbor.

(see Exod. 20:1–17)

THE GREATEST COMMANDMENTS
ACCORDING TO JESUS

"A lawyer asked him a question to test him. 'Teacher, which commandment in the law is the greatest?' He said to him, 'You shall love the Lord your God with all your heart, and with all your soul [*nephesh*, better translated "being"], and with all your mind.'

This is the greatest and first commandment. And a second is like it. 'You shall love your neighbor as yourself.' On these two commandments hang all the law and the prophets" (Matt. 22:35–40). The first commandment comes from Deuteronomy 6:5, the second from Leviticus 19:18.

VARIATIONS OFFERED BY OTHERS

Indigenous American Ten Commandments

1. Treat the Earth and all that dwell thereon with respect.
2. Remain close to the Great Spirit at all times.
3. Always show great respect for your fellow beings.
4. Work together for the benefit of all humankind.
5. Give assistance and kindness wherever needed.
6. Do what you know to be right.
7. Look after the well-being of mind and body.
8. Dedicate a share of your efforts to the greater good.
9. Be truthful and honest at all times.
10. Take full responsibility for your actions.[7]

Universal Laws

1. No planet damage.
2. No body damage.
3. No lying.
4. No stealing.
5. No abandonment.
6. No enslavement.
7. No rape.
8. No murder.
9. No death wars.[8]

7. See online *www.angelfire.com/tx/carolynegenealogy/native10.html*
8. Wolf von Bergstedt, "Code of Ethics," *The Tennessean*, March 4, 2005, 11A.

WHICH VIEW FOR YOU?

Which view of God is authoritative for you?

> Then the Lord said, "I have observed the misery of my people who are in Egypt; I have heard their cry on account of their taskmasters. Indeed, I know their sufferings, and I have come down to deliver them from the Egyptians." (**Moses**, in Exodus 3:7–8)

Through these words Moses and the Israelites perceived God to be a God of justice and compassion who called them to form an alternative community based on justice and compassion.

> Thus says the Lord of hosts, "I will punish the Amalekites for what they did in opposing the Israelites when they came out of Egypt. Now go and attack Amalek, and utterly destroy all that they have; do not spare them, but kill both man and woman, child and infant, ox and sheep, camel and donkey." (**Samuel** speaking to Saul in 1 Samuel 15:2–3)

Through these words the Israelites perceived God to be a God of violence and revenge who justified genocide.

Which view of women is authoritative for you?

> There is no longer Jew or Greek, there is no longer slave or free, there is no longer male and female, for all of you are one in Christ Jesus. (**Paul**, in Galatians 3:27–29).

This was an important statement supporting women's equality in the early church.

> Let a woman learn in silence with full submission. I permit no woman to teach or to have authority over a man; she is to keep silent. (The **author of 1 Timothy** 2:11–15)

By this time, the male privileges of religion, class, and caste had reasserted themselves in the church, and teachings biased against women were once again proclaimed as the Word of God.

Which view of slavery is authoritative for you?

Tell slaves to be submissive to their masters and to give satisfaction in every respect; they are not to talk back, not to pilfer, but to show complete and perfect fidelity, so that in everything they may be an ornament to the doctrine of God our Savior. (The **author of the letter to Titus** 2:9–10)

I am sending [Onesimus] back to you . . . so that you might have him back forever, no longer as a slave but more than a slave, a beloved brother . . . both in the flesh and in the Lord. (**Paul** in his letter to Philemon 1:12–16).

Which view of Sodom's sin is authoritative for you?

The men of the city, the men of Sodom, both young and old, all the people to the last man, surrounded [Lot's] house; and they called to Lot, "Where are the men who came to you tonight? Bring them out to us, so that we may know them" (Gen. 19:4–6).

Raping male strangers, foreigners, and prisoners of war was a way of degrading and dehumanizing them; in this case, an act of aggressive inhospitality.

Lot went out of the door to the men, shut the door after him, and said, "I beg you, my brothers, do not act so wickedly. Look, I have two daughters who have not known a man; let me bring them out to you, and do to them as you please; only do nothing to these men, for they have come under the shelter of my roof" (Gen. 19:6–8).

A wife and daughters were considered by a man to be his property.

This was the guilt of your sister Sodom: she and her daughters had pride, excess of food, and prosperous ease, but did not aid the poor and needy. They were haughty, and did abominable things before me; therefore I removed them when I saw it. (Ezek. 16:49–50)

Which view of international relations is authoritative for you?

> He shall judge between the nations,
> and shall arbitrate for many peoples;
> they shall beat their swords into plowshares,
> and their spears into pruning hooks;
> nation shall not lift up sword against nation,
> neither shall they learn war anymore.
>   (Isa. 2:4)

> Proclaim this among the nations:
> Prepare war,
> stir up the warriors.
> Let all the soldiers draw near,
> let them come up.
> Beat your plowshares into swords,
> and your pruning hooks into spears;
> let the weakling say, "I am a warrior."
>   (Joel 3:9–10)

These various passages are good examples of how one can go to the Bible and cherry-pick verses to provide "authority" for almost any kind of thought and behavior.

MEN ARE FROM MARS...

Most of the Bible reflects a patriarchal viewpoint. Men are the primary actors and the primary interpreters of what God is saying. One of the most disturbing examples of this can be found in Genesis 22:1–24, in the story of the near-sacrifice of Isaac: "God tested Abraham . . . 'Take your son, your only son Isaac, whom you love, and go to the land of Moriah, and offer him there as a burnt offering on one of the mountains that I shall show you.' "

Whether Abraham heard God correctly and whether God would ever test a person this way are serious theological problems. Apparently Abraham was influenced by the piety of some of the pagans around him who believed that infant sacrifice was acceptable or appreciated by their gods. It is regrettable that he was not able to check out this hearing of God's word in a community of faith, and especially with its closest member, his wife. If one were to consider Sarah, the story might have been written quite differently.

A RE-VISIONING OF SARAH

What if the story of Abraham and Isaac were told through Sarah's eyes and heart? Ellen Umansky imagines how this must have been for Sarah: "It was morning. Sarah had just awakened and reached over to touch her husband, Abraham, to caress him, but Abraham wasn't there. Neither, she discovered, was Isaac, her only son, Isaac, whom she loved more than anyone or anything in the world." After dressing, Sarah searches for them, but discovers that they're gone — along with Abraham's ass and his two young servants.

"Hours passed. It was hot and Sarah thought about going inside to escape the heat of the sun. But what if I miss them, she thought. I want to make sure that I catch the first glimpse of them, even if they're far away. And so she stood and waited... and waited...." Even as the sun set and the air grew colder, she stood there, waiting and wondering nervously about her son, Isaac. This child had been God's gift to her, even when she laughed at God's announcement of her pregnancy, for Sarah's body was old. Her belly and breasts had become full — she had become full of life. But now again she cried, moaning and wailing because she was afraid.

She looked around her and saw the fields, now empty, and in the distance saw the mountains, sloping upwards into the sky. And then she saw them... Abraham walking with his ass and his servants and Isaac far behind, walking slowly, his head turning from side to side, his hands oddly moving as though he were trying to make sense of something, and Sarah knew in that instant where Abraham and Isaac had been and why they had gone. Though she could barely make out the features of Isaac's face, she could tell from his movements and his gestures that he was angry, that he wanted nothing to do with his father who had tried to kill him. Abraham was almost down the mountain by now and soon would be home. He'd try to explain, to make her understand his side of the story. But Sarah wanted no part of it. She was tired of hearing Abraham's excuses and even more tired of hearing what *he* thought God demanded. And so Sarah turned and went inside and prayed that, if only for one night, Abraham would leave her alone.[9]

A "MARY" BAND OF FOLLOWERS

How many women in the Bible can you name? You could probably do better with the names of men! Both the Old and New

---

9. This section is taken from Ellen M. Umansky, "Creating a Jewish Feminist Theology," in *Weaving Visions: New Patterns in Feminist Spirituality*, ed. Judith Plaskow and Carol P. Christ (San Francisco: HarperSanFrancisco, 1989).

Testaments reflect a patriarchal context. Most of their key figures and writers were men. But women were an integral part of the Jesus movement. They provided financial support for Jesus and his followers. They attended his teachings and even taught others themselves. They were present at the crucifixion and the tomb. They were the first to witness the resurrection. Their presence in the folks that followed Jesus was another sign that Jesus and his inclusive group believed that God was placing commas where that patriarchal society was placing periods.

Relatively speaking, among Jesus' female followers were his aunt, Salome, who was also the mother of James and John; Mary, the mother of the disciple James; and Joanna, the wife of Herod's steward, Chuza. Here are some of their references: Luke 8:1–3; Matthew 27:55–56, 57–61; Luke 23:55–24:10; Mark 16:9–11.

WHAT'S MY MALIGN?

"No one whose testicles are crushed or whose penis is cut off shall be admitted to the assembly of the Lord" (Deut. 23:1). This restrictive clause was added to the Purity Code by Jewish legalists who believed God had told them to do so.

Later on, the prophet Isaiah heard a different word. He wrote, "To the eunuchs who keep my Sabbaths, who choose the things that please me and hold fast my covenant, I will give, in my house and within my walls, a monument and a name better than sons and daughters; I will give them an everlasting name that shall not be cut off" (Isa. 56:4–5). You could say that Isaiah heard a still-speaking God using a comma instead of a period.

Now turn to the New Testament and the Book of Acts. There you will read about an Ethiopian eunuch (a black man) riding home in his chariot after visiting the Jerusalem Temple for worship. The author of Acts says that an angel of the Lord sent the disciple Philip to catch up with the eunuch's chariot. When Philip did, he heard the man reading from the scroll of Isaiah. "Do you understand what you are reading?" Philip asked. The eunuch said he did not. Philip told him about the good news of extravagant welcome that Jesus and the disciples had extended to everyone. It was such good news to the eunuch that when the chariot came to some water, the eunuch asked Philip to baptize him. His baptism was a sign of the radical inclusion that Jesus and his followers offered.

> If Philip moved the eunuch to faith in Jesus, didn't that make the eunuch's chariot the first conversion van?

NOT KOSHER?
NOW THERE'S A PICKLE

One afternoon when a hungry Peter was visiting Simon, the tanner, by the seaside at Joppa, Peter went up to the roof to pray (Acts 10:1–48). While he was praying, he fell into a trance and had a vision of birds of prey, reptiles, and four-footed animals set before him as God commanded him to kill them and eat. Peter refused, for the animals before him were not kosher, that is, not considered "clean" by Jewish purity laws. God was insistent and repeated this directive three times. Peter was uncertain what to make of this vision until its meaning arrived at Simon's door. A delegation from Cornelius, a God-fearing Roman centurion, had come, requesting an appointment with Peter.

Peter immediately realized the message of his vision: that God wanted him to witness to the Gentile Cornelius and share the good news with him. "I truly understand," he said, "that God shows no partiality, but in every nation anyone who fears him and does what is right is acceptable to him."

The account in Acts states that the circumcised believers who accompanied Peter to Caesarea were astounded to discover that the gift of the Holy Spirit had been poured out even on the

Gentiles! Recognizing this as a new comma development, Peter baptized Cornelius and also the group of relatives and close friends who had come to hear Peter that day.

FAIL, FAIL, THE GANG'S ALL HERE

Peter's denial of Jesus is a story that is well known and often told. The cock crows and Peter has failed to witness to either his love for Jesus or his discipleship.

But unwinding the story a bit more, we see that the failure of Peter is not the last word. Recall that there were women who did not desert Jesus at the crucifixion. They watched to see where his body was taken. Carrying spices, they went to the tomb to anoint his body. It was these women who encountered the presence of the Risen Christ.

Mark describes these women as following and serving Jesus. These are words used to describe disciples! Moreover, with this disciple-like description, the women were even named: Mary Magdalene, Mary the mother of James, Salome.

It was these women who were told by a young man in a white robe, "Go tell his disciples and Peter that he is going ahead of you to Galilee; there you will see him, just as he told you" (Mark 16:7). Peter's denial was not the end of the story. There was not a period there. Failure to be a good disciple did not remove him eternally from the love of God. God's love for Peter and all of us is offered again and again and the possibilities of growing in grace are continually renewed.

Unfortunately, the women disciples had the same sort of response that the male disciples did. They fled. They were afraid.

Mark's Gospel unfolds a powerful lesson: being a disciple is fraught with struggles, uncertainties, and disappointments. But these are never the end. God forgives. God understands. God continues to call us into service, "to accept the cost and joy of discipleship."

THANK GOD, WE'RE A-PAULED

Paul translated the message of the first-century Jesus movement into a language and movement that the whole world could embrace. He helped establish house churches throughout the Roman Empire and left a legacy that still impacts the church today.

When studying Paul, one of the first things we must do is separate the authentic letters of Paul from those attributed to him. This is an important consideration because the authorship of the books in the Bible is not always clear. Biblical scholars determine authenticity by analyzing differences in style, tone, vocabulary, content, and context.

Thirteen letters in the New Testament are attributed to Paul. According to scholar John Dominic Crossan and others, only seven of those are *certainly* Pauline (Romans, 1 and 2 Corinthians, Galatians, Philippians, 1 Thessalonians, and Philemon.). Three are *probably not* from Paul (2 Thessalonians, Colossians, and Ephesians). And three are *certainly not* from Paul (1 and 2 Timothy and Titus).

Paul's letters were not general letters written for all future centuries. They were letters written to address the needs, questions, and struggles of the faithful in specific circumstances.

Yet in his writings are basic themes. Paul understood grace as God's law-opposing work in the world. He understood faith as not something possessed by a person, but as a person's whole way of living. Consider Romans 3:21–22:

> But now, apart from law, the righteousness of God has been disclosed, and is attested by the law and the prophets, the righteousness of God through faith in Jesus Christ for all who believe. (Note especially the phrase *faith in* Jesus Christ.)

These verses from the New Revised Standard Version translation include a footnote that reads, "Or *through the faith of Jesus Christ.*" The first translation suggests that one must have a correct belief in Jesus Christ. The second suggests that Jesus' life of faithfulness is a model for all of us. In studying Paul, the latter emphasis seems more accurate.

And speaking of footnotes, another crucial footnote appears in Romans 8:28. The verse used in the text reads, "We know that all things work together for good for those who love God." The footnote reads, "In all things God works for good."

Another of Paul's major themes appears when one does a bit of word study from the Greek. The word translated as "righteousness" is better translated as "justice" or "rightness." Paul is deeply concerned about God's justice.

Finally, another theme for Paul is the importance of inclusiveness in the church and world. To the Galatians, he wrote, "There is no longer Jew or Greek, there is no longer slave or free, there is no longer male and female, for all of you are one in Christ Jesus" (Gal. 3:27–29). Later patriarchal writers attempted to dilute or reverse Paul's strong effort to include women as church leaders. Ten of the twenty-seven church leaders mentioned by Paul in his letter to the Roman church were women (Rom. 16:1–15).

> If there is no longer Jew or Greek,
> slave or free, male and female, are
> there shorter Jews and Greeks,
> slaves and free, males and females?

A COMEDY OF ERRORS

Typos have always been the bane of editors and proofreaders. Following are some of the more notorious biblical typos during the past four centuries.

The Placemakers' Bible, 1562 (Geneva Bible) "Blessed are the placemakers [instead of 'peacemakers']: for they shall be called the children of God." (Matt. 5:9)

The Judas Bible, 1611 "Judas" is substituted for "Jesus."
(Matt. 26:36)

The Fool Bible, 1625–49 "The fool hath said in his heart there
is a God [instead of 'no God'.]" (Ps. 14:1) The printers were
fined £3,000 and all copies were suppressed.

The Wicked Bible, 1631: "Thou shalt [instead of 'shalt not']
commit adultery" (Exod. 20:14). The Bible was printed by
Barker and Lucas, the King's printers at Blackfriars. The fine
of £300 helped to ruin the printer.

The More Sea Bible, 1641: "and there was more sea [instead of
'no more sea']." (Rev. 21:1)

The Unrighteous Bible, 1653: "Know ye not that the unrighteous
shall inherit [instead of 'inherit not'] the Kingdom of God?"
(1 Cor. 6:9). "neither yield ye your members as instruments
of righteousness [instead of 'unrighteousness'] unto sin"
(Rom. 6:13)

The Printers Bible, 1702: "Printers [instead of 'princes'] have
persecuted me without cause." (Ps. 119:161)

The "Sin On" Bible, 1716: "Sin on more [instead of 'sin no
more']" (John 5:14). The mistake was not discovered until six
thousand copies had been printed and bound.

The Vinegar Bible, Oxford, 1717: "The parable of the Vinegar [instead of 'Vineyard']." (Chapter heading for Luke 20)

The Denial Bible, Oxford, 1793: "Philip" is substituted for "Peter" as the apostle who should deny Jesus. (Luke 22:34)

The Murderers' Bible, 1801: "These are murderers [instead of 'murmurers']." (Jude 16)

The Lion's Bible, 1804: "but thy son that shall come forth out of thy lions [instead of 'loins']." (1 Kings 8:19)

The "To remain" Bible, 1805: "persecuted him that was born after the spirit to remain, even so it is now" (Gal. 4:29). The words "to remain" were added in error by the compositor. A proofreader had asked the editor about the comma after "spirit," and the editor had penciled his reply ("to remain") in the margin. The mistake was repeated in the 1819 edition.

The Discharge Bible, 1806: "I discharge [instead of 'charge'] thee before God . . . that thou observe these things." (1 Tim. 5:21)

The Standing Fishes Bible, 1806: "And it shall come to pass that the fishes [instead of 'fishers'] shall stand upon it." (Ezek. 47:10)

The Ear to Ear Bible, 1810: "Who hath ears to ear [instead of 'hear'], let him hear." (Matt. 13:43)

The Wife-hater Bible, 1810: "If any man come to me, and hate not his father and mother . . . yea, and his own wife [instead of 'life']." (Luke 14:26)

The "Large Family" Bible, Oxford, 1820: "Shall I bring to the birth and not cease [instead of 'cause'] to bring forth?" (Isa. 66:9)

The Camels' Bible, 1823: "And Rebekah arose, and her camels [instead of 'damsels']." (Gen. 24:61)

— from *Brewer's Dictionary of Phrase & Fable*

WHEN THE BIBLE COMES ALIVE

How does scripture come alive in our midst? A good example of the way this can happen comes from several verses in Ephesians: "[Christ Jesus] is our peace; in his flesh he has made both groups into one and has broken down the dividing wall, that is, the hostility between us. He has abolished the law with its commandments and ordinances, that he might create in himself one new humanity in place of the two, thus making peace" (2:14–15). What does the scripture say in light of our relationship with God? It is instructive to consider this case study:

The United States has been a declared enemy of Cuba since 1959, when that country rejected its dependent status under the United States and moved into a different social, economic, and political value system. The resulting hostilities have included bombings, invasions, and an economic blockade by the United States. How has this major dividing wall between our two countries been bridged?

• In 1979 the Ecumenical Council of Cuba (now the Council of Churches of Cuba) invited the United Church of Christ to send a delegation to visit Cuba and to establish closer ties of fellowship with the life and mission of the church there. The United Church Board for World Ministries and the Council for Christian Social Action chose a nine-person delegation for this trip representing three levels of the UCC — national, conference, and the local church. Since that year, the UCC (through the UCBWM and Wider Church Ministries) has sponsored annual Cuba study seminars (invited by the Cuban Council of Churches), has participated in a number of mission and theological conferences in Cuba, and has hosted visitors from Cuba.

• In 1984 the Church of the Good Shepherd (UCC) in Carbondale, Illinois, established a partner church relationship with Ebenezer Baptist Church in Havana, Cuba. Over the years, this has included visits of members back and forth.

- In 1997 the Twenty-first General Synod of the UCC adopted a resolution celebrating and affirming the partnership with the Council of Churches in Cuba.

- In 2000 the Pleasant Hill Community Church (UCC) in Pleasant Hill, Tennessee, established a partner church relationship with Second Baptist Church in Santiago de Cuba.

- In 2001 the Southeast Conference of the UCC affirmed a partnership with the ecumenical church in Cuba. This ecumenical partnership was seen to have three significant "anchors" in Cuba — three primary connections through which our common life and mission can be explored, broadened, and celebrated: the Council of Churches of Cuba, the Evangelical Theological Seminary of Matanzas, and the Martin Luther King Jr. Memorial Center founded by Ebenezer Baptist Church.

- In 2005 the Circle of Mercy congregation (UCC and Alliance of Baptists) in Asheville, North Carolina, established a partner church relationship with Iglesia Gethsemane in Camagüey.

- In 2007 the Old First Reformed Church in Philadelphia led a Pennsylvania Southeast Conference delegation in establishing a relationship with the Fraternity of Baptists in Cuba.

These are some of the ways that the verses of Ephesians 2:14–15 have come alive in the UCC.

FOUR

Looking at Worship

AISLE BE SEEING YOU

God is worshiped when our faith is active in love. Sometimes that love in action is directed toward our family and friends. God is also worshiped when our faith is active in love for those who are sick, lonely, and grieving; those who are treated unjustly; and those who are in prison. God is worshiped whenever we courageously demand an end to wrongdoing. God is worshiped whenever we hold one another in prayer.

These actions are the work of God's people. Although we tend not to think of these works as liturgy, they in fact are. The word "liturgy" means the work of God's people. Liturgy is more than a service of worship that we experience on a Sunday morning.

69

Corporate worship in the United Church of Christ is predominantly experienced on Sunday mornings in a local church setting. A congregation's liturgy generally consists of hymns, prayers, reading of scriptures, a sermon, offering, blessings, and a benediction. It may include Holy Communion, Baptism, or other rites of the church, and, in many congregations, confession.

The point of corporate worship is to give praise and thanksgiving to God, to ask for God's grace in life, to present to God concerns and struggles, to uphold the community and world in prayer, and to feel the movement of the Spirit for our days and lives. In many congregations, one can experience children's sermons, liturgical dance, instrumental music, banners and sacred artwork, and choral offerings.

In general, the corporate worship experience follows what is known as the lectionary year. Each Sunday is assigned several scriptural texts: one from the Hebrew Scripture (also called the "Old Testament" by some Christians), a psalm, an epistle, and a reading from the Gospel. It is from these texts that the Sunday morning worship service is designed. At its best, the worship service forms a cohesive experience where hymns reflect the scriptures, special music enhances the theme, and the sermon examines and reflects on the scripture's meaning for today.

The schedule of lectionary readings is intended to cover a significant part of the scriptures and enable conversations with colleagues and friends in other denominations who follow the same series. In recent years, some scholars have been critical of the lectionary series, claiming that some of the most important themes of the scriptures are omitted. While the lectionary is intended to guide the preparers of worship, it is not a requirement that these readings be used for worship. Worship themes may deviate from the lectionary as occasions or the Spirit suggest.

THE REASONS FOR THE SEASONS

The Church Year begins with the four Sundays of **Advent** and reflection on what it means to receive Jesus at Christmas. The Advent season is one of soul-searching and anticipation. In some churches Advent wreaths are used to mark the progression of the four Sundays. A candle is lit each week until Christmas when the center or Christ candle is lit. Sometimes scripture verses are read as the candles are lighted. The candles usually represent hope, peace, love, and joy.

The season of **Christmas**, or Christmastide, as it is called, is twelve days long. It is the season when we consider the birth of Jesus and its meaning for the world.

Following Christmas is the season of **Epiphany**. It begins with the Feast of Epiphany on January 6, which celebrates the baptism of Jesus. The season of Epiphany recalls the arrival of the three kings as described in the nativity story. It is a time to reflect on our baptisms and on the ministry of Jesus. In many Hispanic communities, "Three Kings Day" is more important than Christmas day.

Lent begins with Ash Wednesday, a day when the faithful gather to think about what needs to change in their lives. In some churches ashes, made by burning palms left over from Palm Sunday, are placed on the foreheads of those who come to worship. The ashes symbolize an act of penitence and confession. In other congregations the order of worship emphasizes acts of repentance and confession without the imposition of ashes. In any case, Ash Wednesday begins the forty days of Lent. The Sundays during this season are not counted in the forty days, because they, like all Sundays, commemorate the resurrection, though during this season the celebration is somewhat subdued.

Holy Week is observed in a variety of ways in the United Church of Christ. **Palm Sunday** or Passion Sunday begins the week. If celebrated as Palm Sunday, it recalls Jesus' procession into Jerusalem. Recent historical study considers the procession as a counterdemonstration against Pilate's procession into Jerusalem at each Passover season. If observed as Passion Sunday the emphasis is on the final week of Jesus' life.

Following Palm Sunday, many congregations offer **Maundy Thursday** worship. Maundy is the English form of the Latin word meaning "commandment." It recognizes Jesus' new commandment "to love one another even as I have loved you." The worship on this day is intended to help the faithful reflect on servanthood and the Lord's Supper. Sometimes Maundy Thursday is marked with Passover Seder meal celebrations. Sometimes the worship includes footwashing.

Good Friday follows Maundy Thursday. Some congregations have chosen to include the Good Friday readings in their Maundy Thursday service because they do not hold Good Friday services. Good Friday, however, is a significant day for worship. It is a time when we focus on the passion, death, and burial of Jesus. In many communities congregations join together in ecumenical observances of this day. Good Friday is often marked with a Tenebrae service, Tenebrae meaning shadows. This service is characterized by twelve candles, readings, and hymns. With the reading of each scripture passage and the singing of a hymn, a candle is extinguished. The sanctuary is plunged into darkness. The eternal light, or the altar candle, is carried out and the altar Bible is slammed shut to symbolize the tearing of the Temple curtain when Jesus gave his last breath.

Good Friday may be followed by a service of **Easter Vigil**, which begins in darkness and moves to light. It is usually a late night service that commemorates the faithful gathered together seeking strength. They reflect on their baptism and listen for the good word: "He is risen." This same word is spoken on Easter morning when the faithful gathered respond: "He is risen, indeed!"

The season of **Easter** lasts fifty days, including Sundays. On the fiftieth day, Pentecost (meaning fifty) is observed. Pentecost Sunday recognizes the giving of the Holy Spirit and the birth of the church (Acts 2:1–21). The season of **Pentecost** lasts nearly half a year. It is called "ordinary time" because it generally does not have prescribed festive celebrations. It is a time when we hear many stories of the ministry of Jesus and think about growth in the faith.

TINTS THAT HINT

Each of the seasons in the church year is marked by a particular color. The color of the cloths that dress the communion table or altar, the pulpit or lectern, and even the pastor's stole change. (The stole is the long scarf a pastor wears to symbolize the yoke of Christ.)

Some churches do not observe the seasonal colors, but instead use special flower arrangements, weavings, banners, and even sculptures to convey themes. In many instances, pastors wear stoles from other countries to express their solidarity and support for persons struggling for dignity and justice.

In churches that follow a more traditional liturgical year, Advent is marked by purple or blue symbolizing waiting and hope.

Christmas is marked by white signifying light and purity. Epiphany is either white, again for light, or green for growth. The Lenten color is purple to indicate repentance. The color for the Easter season is white signifying the resurrection. The color for Pentecost Sunday is red, which symbolizes the Pentecostal tongues of fire. The season of Pentecost is marked by the color green, again, for growth.

Additionally, red stoles are worn for installations, ordinations, and when the Protestant Reformation is observed on the last Sunday in October.

TWO "DO'S"

What is your definition of a sacrament? In the Protestant tradition, it is a ceremony believed to have been instituted by Jesus. Down through the years the church has viewed sacraments as signs or symbols of a spiritual reality and as special channels of God's grace.

The United Church of Christ recognizes two sacraments in its worship life: Baptism and Holy Communion.

A sprinkling of details

Through the sacrament of Baptism, one becomes a member of Christ's universal church. There are two essential elements in this sacrament: the symbolism of water (either through sprinkling, immersion, or pouring), and the invocation of the Holy Spirit. Through Baptism, Christians are brought into union with Christ, with each other, and with the church of every time and place. Baptism, a once-in-a-lifetime event, is both God's gift and our human response to that gift.

When an infant or young child is baptized, parents and sponsors make promises to nurture the child in the faith. Baptism is not only a personal celebration in the lives of individuals and their families. It is also a central celebration in the life of the local church. Therefore, Baptism should always take place in the presence of a community of faith gathered for public worship. On this occasion the congregation is also called on to make promises to nurture the faith of the child.

In some congregations, a baptismal candle may be lighted from the Paschal, or Easter, candle, signifying the light of Christ that is present in the infant. Families are encouraged to take the baptismal candle home and light it on the anniversary of the infant's baptism, inviting an occasion for discussion on faith and Baptism as the child grows older.

Those who are baptized at an early age are then given an opportunity to participate in a confirmation class and to affirm their baptisms for themselves. Confirmation is not a graduation event. It is a voluntary self-conscious entry into the life and service of the Christian faith.

When an older child or adult is baptized, the vows are to be made by those individuals on their own behalf, again in the presence of a community of faith gathered for public worship. On such occasions, the presence of water can suggest the additional symbolism of drowning or dying to an old self and a rising to new life in Christ. The vows can also express the intention to participate in the mission and ministry of Jesus.

The order for Baptism from the UCC *Book of Worship* includes a Prayer of Baptism that extends the more traditional prayer to include women and people on the margins of society. You may wish to read it yourself:

> We thank you, God, for the gift of creation called forth by your saving Word. Before the world had shape and form, your Spirit moved over the waters. Out of the waters of the deep, you formed the firmament and brought forth the earth to sustain all life.
>
> In the time of Moses, your people Israel passed through the Red Sea waters from slavery to freedom and crossed the flowing Jordan to enter the promised land.

In the fullness of time, you sent Jesus Christ, who was nurtured in the water of Mary's womb. Jesus was baptized by John in the water of the Jordan, became living water to a woman at the Samaritan well, washed the feet of the disciples and sent them forth to baptize all nations by water and the Holy Spirit.

At whatever age one joins Christ's church universal, the occasion is a glad one and part of a life journey of seeking to be faithful.

THE ELEMENTS AND THE PERIODIC TABLE

The United Church of Christ celebrates the spiritual presence of Jesus in our communal meal of bread and wine or grape juice. The meal of remembrance recalls Jesus' life and passion but also celebrates his continuing presence among his people. Told by Christ to remember him in this meal, we continue the tradition of the early church by sharing in the breaking of the bread and the pouring out of the cup, reminding ourselves that God is forgiving and gracious, empowering and loving. Holy Communion also provides the occasion to remember those with whom we have shared our journeys of faith. Communion points to the possibilities of transformation in our own lives and in the world.

Although the historical norm for Sunday worship suggested in the UCC *Book of Worship* is to include scripture readings, preaching, and Holy Communion, few congregations actually keep this practice. In the United Church of Christ, each congregation determines its own worship practices and customs. There is much discussion today about the frequency of observing Holy Communion.

The manner of Holy Communion also varies. Wine and/or grape juice may be served. Bread of various types or commercial wafers may be used. Wine and bread are sometimes provided by winemakers and breadbakers from within the faith community. In some celebrations of Holy Communion, participants are served the elements in the pew, a practice that places emphasis on the unity of the body of Christ in celebrating the meal. In other churches, participants come to the table to kneel or stand and receive the elements. Commonly, when this is done, the manner of communion is called intinction and refers to the dipping of the bread into a cup of wine/juice. In some congregations, participants come forward to receive the wine/juice in individual cups. When the people are asked to come forward to receive the elements, a stronger emphasis is placed on the individual to respond to God's invitation to remember Jesus and receive God's gifts.

TWO SONGS DON'T MAKE A RITE

A story is told about a young couple planning their wedding. One of the songs they wanted as part of their wedding ceremony was, "I'd Rather Have Jesus." Another was "Turn Back, O Man, Forswear Thy Foolish Ways!" Obviously, these two songs would not make a rite.

A rite is an important ceremony in the life of the church that was not instituted by Jesus. Confirmation, marriage, and ordination, for example, are three rites that many people think of as very special ceremonies of the faith. Indeed, they are.

Confirmation, or Affirmation of Baptism, follows a time of study, reflection, and prayer when one claims for one's own the intent of one's baptism: the following of Christ and the assumption of Christ's mission of love and justice. In most UCC congregations this happens between the ages of thirteen and fifteen. Upon confirmation, individuals are considered adult members of a local congregation.

Marriage is also an important rite in the United Church of Christ. It celebrates the happy moment when two people exchange covenantal promises to be husband and wife. Today, many UCC congregations are rethinking the role of the pastor as an agent of the government in performing marriages that assume legal status. Some in the UCC are refusing to participate in the governmental role, offering instead the blessing of the church through the rite of marriage. This was the model of marriage first practiced in the early years of this country.

Ordination, too, is a special ceremony. It is a commitment for those who have been called by God into service of Word and Sacrament. Entrusted to them are the primary responsibilities for preaching, teaching, administration of sacraments, pastoral care, and leadership. How do folks know when God has called them to such a ministry? Candidates for ordination feel God's call in many ways. Most will describe an urgency to serve that will not let go. These individuals meet with their local church pastor and the Church and Ministry Committee of their Association to investigate the authenticity of their call, their gifts for ministry, and their support for taking on the mantle of these responsibilities. While it is considered ideal for persons ordained to have graduated from college and seminary, the shortage of pastors in some areas of our country has necessitated exceptions to this rule.

Our denomination is at its best when it honors and appreciates the callings and gifts of each member. Though not all are called to ordained ministry, all are called to serve in the priesthood of all believers. Therefore, rites that install elected leaders as well as commission lay leaders for particular service are common in the UCC.

Other rites are unfolding as our denomination grows in theological understandings and faithful practices. Many congregations will now bless same-gender relationships with Rites of Holy Union, though some are advocating that a rite of Holy Union is not necessary because the rite of marriage itself should be offered to those same-gender couples. Some congregations also offer rites for healing, for reconciliation, and for the dissolution of marriage. These are offered in our UCC *Book of Worship*.

LOOKING SHARP!

In 1995, the United Church of Christ published *The New Century Hymnal.* Charged by General Synod XI to produce a collection of hymns and psalms from which no one would be excluded, the hymnal committee sought input from the great diversity of the United Church of Christ.

Included in the hymnal are 617 hymns, some old and some new. The collection broadly includes a variety of meters, styles, and multi-ethnic treasures. Scattered throughout the book are songs in multiple languages: Dakota, Japanese, Samoan, Hawaiian, Spanish, French, German, and more. There are songs for every part of the church year, for opening and closing worship, for the celebration of the sacraments, and for church rites like confirmation, marriage, and installations.

No effort was spared to revise the language of older hymns that formerly relied heavily on militaristic, sexist, or racist terms. Sensitivity was also shown for those congregations who do not have at their disposal professional musicians, for many of the accompaniments are simple. Several of the hymns include guitar chords and descants, making it suitable for different kinds of adaptations and settings.

Nowhere does the great gift of this hymnal become more apparent than when one is worshiping at General Synod. While an individual may not easily sing an unfamiliar language, the multi-ethnic, multi-racial, multi-experience gathering at General Synod sings with power and joy.

A NOTABLE GATHERING
OF HYMNS AND HERS

Fifty-three of the 617 hymns in *The New Century Hymnal* have been written by UCC members or UCC forebears — an indication of a longtime denominational interest in hymnody. Following is a listing of our twenty-eight hymn writers and the dates of their words. (In a number of cases, their lyrics have been altered by the Hymnal Committee.)

Nineteenth century

Katharine Lee Bates

> #594 "How Beautiful, Our Spacious Skies" (1893, alt.)

Dakota Hymn

> #3 "Wakantanka Taku Nitawa," adapt. Joseph R. Renville (1842)

Henry Harbaugh

> #457 "Jesus, I Live to You" (1850, alt.)

William W. How

> #315 "O Word of God Incarnate," adapt. (1867) from words by John Robinson

James O'Kelly

> #617 "Unite and Join Your Cheerful Songs" (1816)

Edwin Parker

> #536 "Savior, an Offering Costly and Sweet" (1888, alt.)

Queen's Hymn (Queen Liliuokalani, Hawaii)

> #58 "Spirit of Love," adapt. Shirley Erena Murray (1992)

Jeremiah E. Rankin

#81 "God Be with You" (1880, alt.)

Ernest W. Shurtleff

#573 "Lead on Eternal Sovereign" (1887, alt.)

Twentieth century (first half)

Purd E. Deitz

#607 "We Would Be Building" (1935, alt.)

Robert Nawahine

#496 "Ekolu Mea Nui" ("Three Greatest Things") (faith, hope, aloha)

Henry Hallam Tweedy

#263 "O Spirit of the Living God" (1933, alt.)

Howard Arnold Walter

#492 "I Would Be True" (1917)

Twentieth century (second half)

Lavon Bayer

#170 "Your Ways Are Not Our Own" (1988, rev. 1993)

#174 "Hear the Voice of God, So Tender" (1987, rev. 1993)

#215 "Ride On! Ride On in Majesty" (adapt. 1993)

#312 "We Love Your Realm, O God" (adapt. 1992)

#421 "We Gather Together" (adapt. 1992)

#479 "God Is My Shepherd" (adapt. 1992)

#615 "Enter in the Realm of God" (1994)

Curtis Beach

#8 "Praise to the Living God" (1966, alt.)

#558 "O How Glorious, Full of Wonder" (1958, alt., rev. 1980)

David Beebe

#461 "Let Us Hope when Hope Seems Hopeless" (1989)

Dosia Carlson

#179 "We Yearn, O Christ, for Wholeness" (1986, rev. 1993)

#560 "By Whatever Name We Call You" (1990)

#574 "In Egypt under Pharaoh" (1989)

Al Carmines

#177 "God of Change and Glory" (1973)

Arthur G. Clyde

#112 "Keep Awake, Be Always Ready" (1993)

Ronald Cole-Turner

#325 "Child of Blessing, Child of Promise" (1981)

James W. Crawford

#47 "O Christ Jesus, Sent from Heaven" (1994)

Ruth Duck

#30 "Colorful Creator" (1992)

#36 "To God Compose a Song of Joy" (1986)

#106 "My Heart Sings Out with Joyous Praise" (1985)

#110 "Now Bless the God of Israel" (1985)

#164 "Arise, Your Light Is Come" (1973)

#168 "O Radiant Christ, Incarnate Word" (1989)

#274 "Womb of Life, and Source of Being" (1986, 1990)

#343 "Jesus Took the Bread" (1982)

#357 "You Are Called to Tell the Story" (1991)

#376 "God We Thank You for Our People" (1986)

#439 "A Mighty Fortress Is Our God" (adapt. 1981)

#521 "In Solitude" (1983)

#554 "Out of the Depths, O God, We Call" (1988)

#563 "We Cannot Own the Sunlit Sky" (1984, rev. 1989)

William Gay

#435 "Each Winter as the Year Grows Older" (1969, alt.)

James Gertmenian

#20 "God of Abraham and Sarah" (1986, alt.)

#464 "The Weaver's Shuttle Swiftly Flies" (1990)

Paul R. Gregory

#538 "Standing at the Future's Threshold" (1985, rev. 1994)

James L. Haddix

#426 "O God, Whose Steadfast Love" (1986, rev. 1994)

Richard D. Leach

#201 "An Outcast among Outcasts" (1992)

#206 "A Woman Came Who Did Not Count the Cost" (1990)

James K. Manley

#286 "Spirit, Spirit of Gentleness" (1978, alt.)

James F. D. Martin

#114 "Return, My People" (1981, alt.)

#313 "Like a Tree beside the Waters" (1992)

Marion M. Meyer

#69 "Come God, Creator, Be Our Shield" (1990)

Deborah Patterson

#368 "Sheltered by God's Loving Spirit" (1991)

Phil Porter

#335 "Come, Gather in This Special Place" (1991)

HYMNING AND AWEING

There are many old and new treasures in *The New Century Hymnal*. Many of them are related to the UCC's attention to the cross, crown, and world. Although the UCC's use of the comma as a symbol developed after the hymnal's publication in 1995, there are hymns in it that address the good news that a comma-placing God has a further word for us beyond our finalities and periods.

Two examples of these both describe a God of *surprises* — One who surprises us with good news that there is still more to the story. The first is "Who Would Think That What Was Needed" by John Bell, Graham Maul, and the Iona Community (#153, written in 1990), and the second, "I Was There to Hear Your Borning Cry" by John Ylvisaker (#351, written in 1985).

SINGING GOD'S EXTRAVAGANT WELCOME

Here's a wonderful gathering song that is not in *The New Century Hymnal*. The words and music are by James K. Manley, a UCC minister. (The music can be ordered directly from him.)[1]

Part of the Family

Refrain:
> Come in, come in and sit down,
> you are a part of the family.
> We are lost and we are found,
> and we are a part of the family.

Verses:

1. You know the reason why you came,
   yet no reason can explain;
   so share in the laughter and cry in the pain,
   for we are a part of the family.

---

1. Words and music by James K. Manley; arr. DN, © 1984 by James K. Manley, 747 Plymouth Rd., Claremont, CA 91711. 909-624-5069. *www.manleymusic.com*. Used by permission.

God is with us in this place,
like a mother's warm embrace.
We're all forgiven by God's grace,
for we are a part of the family.

2. Children and elders, middlers and teens,
singles and doubles and in-betweens,
strong eighty-fivers and streetwise sixteens,
for we are a part of the family.
Greeters and shoppers, longtime and new,
nobody here has a claim on a pew;
and whether we're many or whether we're few,
we are a part of the family.

3. There's a life to be shared in the bread and the wine;
we are the branches, Christ is the vine.
This is God's temple, it's not yours or mine,
but we are a part of the family.
There's rest for the weary and health for us all,
there's a yoke that is easy, and a burden that's small.
So come in and worship and answer the call,
for we are a part of the family.

OH GIVE ME A HOME
WITH THE WORDS OF SHALOM

How do you think of God? As a spirit? A father? A warrior? A
king? In the Bible, there are also feminine images of God: as a
female eagle teaching the eaglet to fly (Deut. 32:11), as a mother
giving birth (Isa. 42:14), as a woman keeping house (Luke 15:8–
10), as a nursing mother (Isa. 49:15a). Different images expand
or contract our faith experience. For many, it is essential to have
different images and ways of speaking of God in order that we not
commit idolatry. After all, God is beyond any name that can be
ascribed to God. This is the challenge of inclusive language.

When one considers the whole process of naming, there is also an element of power that enters into the equation. Remember Adam naming the animals? (Gen. 2:19). That story tells us that Adam was the ruler of his domain.

In Isaiah God says, "...I have called you by name, you are mine" (Isa. 43:1b). How has God named us? As a child of God, as a woman of faith, a man of faith, as a follower, a leader, a pastor, a teacher? Each of the ways that we are named highlights some important aspect of our character.

Similarly, each name for God emphasizes different aspects of the God who will never fully be known. Indeed, we worship a God who continues to speak in commas, not periods.

What about our language for human beings then? That, too, presents problems. Our everyday language reinforces what we think of one another. Are we being seen as too young or too old? Are we defined by a disability or challenge as some earlier translations of Bible stories do when they describe the crippled and the blind? Are we only seen by the color of our skin or the gender expressions we share with the world? For if we are seen in some sort of caricature, then we are acting unjustly toward one another. Nothing about our speech, in that case, liberates. Nothing includes. Nothing honors.

That is the concern of inclusive language: that all of God's people are honored for the gifts that they are and the sensitivities that they bring to our communities of faith and to our world.

Looking at the accessibility of our God language and human descriptions has opened up another great gift: other ways we may be accessible. Ramps and elevators, large print bulletins, special Sunday School classes for children with autism, hearing devices for those who require amplification, American Sign Language interpreters for those whose primary language is sign, and many more responses have made our church communities richer for the inclusion of a greater variety of persons.

But our work is not done. As long as there are some who feel excluded, as long as there are some treated with injustice, as long as there are some wounded by our insensitivities, we are not living the shalom of Jesus.

GLORY DAYS

Remember those children's books with the horizontally divided pages? You could put the head of a donkey on the body of an alligator with the legs of a duck. It made all sorts of funny pictures. Sometimes worship can feel like it has been put together by the same folks who designed those children's books. But it doesn't have to be that way. With a little guidance from a pastor, designing worship can be a very meaningful activity for members of a congregation.

Does your congregation have a worship committee? Are there people in your church who help plan the worship service? Many congregations do have people involved in a wide variety of ways:

Banner makers, parament weavers, and chancel decorators

Liturgical dancers

Chancel musicians: vocal and instrumental

Choirs

Readers and lectors

Artists

Audio visual operators

Children's sermon folks

Communion assistants

Drama players

"Mission Moment" folks

Ushers

Greeters

Bread bakers

Winemakers

Acolytes

Bell ringers

Worship may be formal or informal. It is just as valid in a park as a sanctuary. It may be led by a pastor or by lay members, by adults or by youth. It may concentrate on a theme like Youth Sunday or Earth Day. It may follow the suggested lectionary readings.

Sometimes worship comforts with the familiar, sometimes it stretches with something new. It may include unusual actions like footwashing or handwashing. It may introduce different breads for Communion (whole wheat, rye, pita, flat bread, pan fry bread, tortillas).

How is a service of worship planned? Each congregation in the United Church of Christ answers that question for itself.

One thing is certain: the more that people are invited to participate in the planning of worship, the more they understand what is happening in worship. Involving a worship committee can revitalize a congregation that seems stuck going through the motions. And as people participate in the actual worship service itself, they may well find that they are more connected with the scripture readings, the theme, the anthems that may be sung, and the prayers that are prayed.

Designing a worship service that is cohesive takes practice. Worship themes expand with the careful selection of calls to worship, invocations, prayers, hymns, anthems, children's sermons, etc. Once a faithful effort has been made, one simply has to trust the Spirit to do the rest. Many times the results are surprising.

Finally, as you plan worship, your church may discover that there are needs that are not being met on Sunday morning. Perhaps a service of corporate worship could be added on another day. If your church has a number of members who are gone in the summer, why not offer a worship service that is not on the weekend. If your church seems to empty out in the winter, why not think of ways to make your sanctuary experience feel more intimate for a smaller group of people?

The United Church of Christ has a marvelous history of creative worship. Being creative is a comma activity.

FIVE

Looking at Our Structure

COVENANTAL CONNECTION

In all aspects of its institutional life, the United Church of Christ is covenantally bound. Our local churches, area Associations, regional Conferences, and national General Synod all work together in a covenantal relationship.

The concept of covenant is reflected in many cultures, but in our own faith history it is reflected directly in the divine-human relationship affirmed by our spiritual ancestors at Mount Sinai. In this covenant, Yahweh and the Israelites (Exod. 20ff.) would relate together beyond traditional notions of "promise" or "agreement," both of which can easily be broken.

A covenantal relationship is one in which both parties are responsible to one another and neither is dictated to by the other.

While God handed down laws from Mount Sinai along with many expectations, God could not compel obedience. The Israelites, who spent much of their history both listening to and running from the God who had claimed them, discovered that honoring the covenantal relationship brought well-being and shalom, while ignoring the covenant led to chaos and finally exile.

Yet the biblical covenant did not end with the Babylonian exile. God "remembered Israel's injustice and idolatry no more" (Isa. 65:17) and called Israel back into relationship. Israel re-engaged with their God and their story to go forth once again in faith and in the hope that there would be newness and joy in their future. When God is in the center of the covenant, such relationships never end.

What does this relationship mean to us in the United Church of Christ? While we honor local church "autonomy," our covenantal understanding is at the center of our being UCC. The national church structure depends upon local churches for financial support. Local churches look to national, regional, and area ministries in turn, to strengthen their ability to spread the Gospel within their local communities and to reach out to the world. This is done through educational materials, workshops, and the preparation of resources for local church ministers. Further, national church bodies and ministries can speak and act on their own behalf in relation to critical national and global issues such as war, poverty, or environmental concerns, and local congregations can do the same.

In our denomination the local church cannot do its work without the help of its regional and national entities. Likewise, and perhaps more importantly, the larger ministries of the UCC cannot even exist without the covenantal support of the local church.

In the UCC we believe that God's realm is always closer to fruition when the human family is struggling and striving together. Our covenantal relationships are both an affirmation of God's centrality in our life together, and a witness against a world that consistently places individualism and autonomy above the needs of the community.

LET'S ASSOCIATE!

In the United Church of Christ the local congregation makes its own decisions. Questions of who shall pastor, who will be hired as church professionals, how often Communion will be celebrated, the manner in which it will be celebrated, whether or not the lectionary series will be followed, whether or not children will be baptized, and a host of other questions are the prerogative of the local church.

While the local church exercises great autonomy, it is in covenant with the denomination by virtue of the fact that it accepted the UCC preamble to the constitution. What exactly was that? Good question. Keep reading.

The United Church of Christ acknowledges as its sole Head, Jesus Christ, Son of God and Savior. It acknowledges as kindred in Christ all who share in this confession. It looks to the Word of God in the scriptures, and to the presence and power of the Holy Spirit, to prosper its creative and redemptive work in the world. It claims as its own the faith of the historic Church expressed in the ancient creeds and reclaimed in the basic insights of the Protestant Reformers. It affirms the responsibility of the Church in each generation to make this faith its own in reality of worship, in honesty of thought and expression, and in purity of heart before God. In accordance with the teaching of our Lord and the practice prevailing among evangelical Christians, it recognizes two sacraments: Baptism and the Lord's Supper, or Holy Communion.

It was this declaration that congregations affirmed when they joined together as the United Church of Christ. In joining they agreed to covenant with one another to accept and respect the ministry of each part of our denomination; that is, of local church, Associations, Conferences, and General Synod, and our general and wider church ministries. The strength of our covenant with one another is the strength of our wider church as God has called us through new occasions to learn new duties.

UCC SEMINARIES

The United Church of Christ has a historic relationship with eight seminaries that continue to provide leadership in the training of racial and ethnic leaders.

Hartford Seminary
77 Sherman Street
Hartford, CT 06105
860-509-9500
www.hartsem.edu

Harvard University Divinity School
45 Francis Avenue
Cambridge, MA 02138
617-495-5761
www.hds.harvard.edu

Howard University School of Divinity
1400 Shepherd Street NE
Washington, DC 20017
202-806-0500
www.howard.edu/divinity

Interdenominational Theological Center
671 Beckwith Street SW
Atlanta, GA 30314
404-527-7792
www.itc.edu

Seminario Evangélico de Puerto Rico
776 Ponce de León Avenue
San Juan PR 00925-2207
787-763-6700
www.seminarioevangelicopr.org/home.htm

Union Theological Seminary
3041 Broadway at Reinhold Niebuhr Place
New York, NY 10027
212-280-1317
www.utsnyc.edu

Vanderbilt University Divinity School
Nashville, TN 37240
www.vanderbilt.edu/divinity

Yale University Divinity School
409 Prospect Street
New Haven, CT 06511
203-432-5303
www.yale.edu/divinity

The United Church of Christ has seven seminaries. These seminaries are schools of the church, called to strengthen and support the life and mission of the church by educating pastors and teachers, enlivening critical reflection on faith, and encouraging Christian discipleship. Following is a list of the seven:

Andover Newton Theological School
210 Herrick Rd.
Newton Centre, MA 02459-2243
(617) 964-1100
www.ants.edu

Bangor Theological Seminary
2 College Circle
P.O. Box 44
Bangor, ME 04401-0411
(207) 942-6781
www.bts.edu

Chicago Theological Seminary
5757 S. University Ave.
Chicago, IL 60657-1507
(773) 752-5757
www.ctschicago.edu

Eden Theological Seminary
475 E. Lockwood Ave.
St. Louis, MO 63119
(314) 961-3627
www.eden.edu

Lancaster Theological Seminary
555 W. James St.
Lancaster, PA 17603-2897
(717) 393-0654
www.lts.org

Pacific School of Religion
1798 Scenic Ave.
Berkeley, CA 94709
(510) 848-0528
www.psr.edu

United Theological Seminary of the Twin Cities
3000 5th St. NW
New Brighton, MN 55112
(651) 633-4311
www.unitedseminary.edu

RIGHT ON CUE

Chicago, United, and Eden Seminaries realized that rather than compete with one another they could accomplish more by joining together to solicit financial support. CUE (Chicago, United, Eden) is the result of their effort. Over two thousand congregations donate to the combined seminary educational fund of these three seminaries. The CUE program raised approximately 7–8 percent of the cost of seminary education.

PROCLAIM THE AIM

The United Church of Christ has a number of designations that congregations can adopt to describe themselves on their journey to justice and shalom — designations that indicate how they see themselves participating in Jesus' life and mission in the world today.

By identifying itself as a **Whole Earth Church**, a congregation publicly declares that the earth and all the created world call for compassion and care from its members. Claiming such a label would invite folks in your community and beyond your community to see your faith lived out in love as you care for the earth, its waters and air, and all its inhabitants.

Perhaps on that journey to justice and shalom, you identify another deep desire: to be a Just Peace Church. Proclaiming your intention to be a **Just Peace Church** is an invitation to marginalized and oppressed people that they and their concerns are welcome in this community of believers. It is a commitment that this community of faithful will not shrink from the calling to be channels of God's love and justice in the individual and systemic work that is needed today or the challenges that will arise tomorrow.

Jesus' life and ministry reflected the extravagant welcome that God extends to everyone, and this is an important part of the UCC's life and ministry also. How do you let your community know that your congregation is particularly sensitive to gay men, lesbians, bisexual and transgender persons? What if it were important to you that your congregation be seen as a ray of hope in the GLBT struggle? The answer is, declare your church to be an **Open and Affirming** congregation. Join the more than seven hundred congregations denomination-wide that see this designation as a necessary step on a journey to justice and shalom.

Still another affirmation of congregational identity is found among those churches that have made themselves and declared themselves to be **Accessible to All**. These churches have sought to make sure that no one is excluded because of physical or social barriers.

Finally, some congregations are witnessing to their intention to be **Multi-racial** and **Multi-cultural**. They are including bilingual worship and special programming to extend their outreach.

Proclaiming the aim invites others on your journey of faith as you accept the cost and joy of discipleship in the work to which you have been called. But be aware. Once you have declared your intention to be about this work, God will take your pledge very seriously.

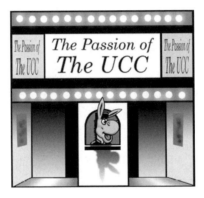

SUPPORT FOR OUR JOURNEY

The United Church of Christ has its national headquarters in Cleveland, Ohio. What kind of work does a headquarters do? Direct? Mandate? Advise? Support? Resource? Quarterback?

For a denomination that has sought to meld two very different organizational backgrounds — the local church and corporate board autonomy of the Congregational Christian Churches and the more connectional approach of the Evangelical and Reformed Church — the organizational structuring has been a "work in progress." Both local church autonomy and denominational connectionalism have been incorporated into the UCC structure.

The basic power and decision-making in the UCC lies in the representative General Synod that meets every two years, and in the Executive Council that meets in between. The ongoing resourcing and "quarterbacking" of the UCC has been carried out through four national ministries based at the headquarters in Cleveland. Following are their mission statements:

"The purpose and mission of the **Office of General Ministries** shall be to care for the spiritual life, unity, and well-being of the church; to nurture its covenantal life and its ecumenical and interfaith relationships; to provide regular processes which focus on theological reflection throughout the church; and to facilitate the visioning, planning, coordination, and implementation of the total mission of the United Church of Christ."

General Ministries includes the office of the UCC General Minister and President (who traditionally embodies a pastoral and prophetic role on behalf of the UCC), associate ministers, and concerns for UCC proclamation, identity, and communication, and financial development.

"The purpose and mission of **Justice and Witness Ministries** of the United Church of Christ shall be to embrace God's transforming mission to do justice, seek peace, and build community. Therefore, in response to the call of Christ, we speak and act prophetically through public witness, policy advocacy, issue education, and grassroots empowerment to build a more just, compassionate and inclusive world."

Various program teams are based in Cleveland, Washington, DC, and Whitakers, North Carolina.

"The purpose and mission of the **Local Church Ministries** shall be to encourage and support local churches of the United Church of Christ in the fulfillment of God's mission."

Concerns in this section include congregational vitality, evangelism, church development and renewal, parish life and leadership, publications and resources, stewardship and church finances, worship and education.

"The purpose and mission of **Wider Church Ministries** shall be to encourage and support local Churches, Associations, and national expressions of the United Church of Christ to participate in the global, multiracial, multicultural church, accessible to all; to support United Church of Christ ministries around the world and the nation; and to plan and conduct common global ministries with the Christian Church (Disciples of Christ)."

Concerns in this section include mission education and interpretation, global advocacy and education, global sharing of resources, health and wholeness advocacy, child sponsorship, partner relations, mission personnel, and overseas ministries.

TAKING STOCK: THE PENSION BOARDS

The United Church of Christ has an affiliated ministry that extends care and support to retired and active laity and clergy in the denomination. The Pension Boards are composed of two nonprofit corporations: The Pension Boards–United Church of Christ, Ind., and United Church Board for Ministerial Assistance, Inc.

These Boards wrestle with investing in companies that best reflect the justice concerns of the denomination and insuring the future needs of pensioners. They continue to be challenged to reflect the support of the denomination for gay, lesbian, and transgender persons and their partners.

VOLUNTEER OPPORTUNITIES

Have you ever thought about doing something special for a year or a summer or even a few weeks? The United Church of Christ has many opportunities for youth and adults all across the United States and Puerto Rico. Skills and requirements vary by the opportunity. To find out more, check out *www.ucc.org.*

In the United Church of Christ you can volunteer through Global Ministries or the UCC Volunteer Ministries. If you volunteer with Global Ministries you can get involved with mission

trips, mission work, and supporting mission work here at home. This is a wonderful opportunity for youth, young adults, those in or considering seminary and other special groups.

Volunteer Ministries also offers many summer opportunities for students and other possibilities of shorter or longer duration. You could work in maintenance or with livestock at the Heifer Project International ministry in Perryville, Arkansas. If you are twenty-one or older you could work with runaway youth in Chicago. Perhaps you are called to work with people who have developmental disabilities. If so, you may find your niche at Emmaus Homes and Emmaus Homes, Inc., in St. Charles and Marthasville, Missouri. In Atlanta volunteers are needed to work with prisoners in the Open Door Community. In that case you would live as a residential advisor and live and work with community members and participate in a prison ministry program at Central Georgia Prison. How about helping formerly homeless folks who are coping with mental illness? If that ministry calls you, you could find yourself working in Seattle, Washington, at the Plymouth House of Healing. And these are just a sampling of the volunteer work that is available through the United Church of Christ.

There really are many ways to serve. You may find that in being a blessing to others, you are greatly blessed. Be aware that there are deadlines for applications. Check out the details.

PUBLISHED GLAD TIDINGS

The *United Church News* is the official denominational newspaper of the United Church of Christ. It is published bimonthly by the Proclamation, Identity, and Communication Ministry, which is part of the Office of General Ministries of our church.

In many conferences the *United Church News* comes with a conference wrap-around section, which contains news especially for the conference, associations, and local congregations. The bimonthly publication is available free, but contributions are much appreciated. Checks can be sent to United Church News, P.O. Box 247, Bellmawr, NJ 08099-0247.

The paper includes articles examining current activities in the denomination, letters to the editor, news reports, Bible study, spirituality articles, classifieds, and stories relating to General Synod pronouncements and resolutions. It often includes articles about particular congregations and their imaginative ways of being environmentally green, accessible to all, embracing of the poor and dispossessed, and trumpeting the justice work being done in the United Church of Christ. Youth and children, young and older adults all find their way into this newspaper.

It's a good read. Check it out if you haven't already.

"SEND AN OWL?"

In the beginning of this handbook, you learned about the UCC history and its investment in educational institutions throughout our nation. Even today, the importance of education is stressed in our denomination.

As a church, the UCC has developed many fine educational programs for children, teens, confirmands, and adults. Some programs follow the lectionary readings and are easily incorporated with the themes from Sunday worship. Others, like "Our Whole Lives" (OWL) are special focus educational offerings for youth. In this case, OWL is an educational program on sexuality. Other offerings are for the adults of the church and include a great variety of offerings from questions of faith and Bible study or current events.

As did our church mothers and fathers before us, we value the role of education in equipping us to be active in God's mission and work in the world.

IT'S TIME TO GIVE A RAM

For many people, stewardship is about giving a tithe, or 10 percent of one's income, to a local church. In the United Church of Christ we believe stewardship is about every decision we make. How are we good stewards of our relationships, our homes, our planet, our gardens, our schools, our unique gifts?

In Genesis 2 Adam is given the power to name the animals. A caretaking relationship with the earth is begun. It is a relationship that suggests power and responsibility.

There are other stewardship stories in the Bible. These stories emphasize care for household goods, vineyards, and fields. They come with injunctions to care for the widow, the orphan, and alien. What does this mean for us today?

The United Church of Christ wrestles with this question as it seeks to see the world and humanity through a vision that is inspired by Jesus. To the powerless, Jesus gave compassion. He healed the sick and reached out to the poor. He welcomed those who had been shunned. In his actions and teachings, he inspired his followers to work for justice and equity for all people.

Therefore the UCC, while engaged in many works of charity, is also concerned about acting to address the **causes** of injustice. *Why* is a person hungry? *Why* is a person sick? *Why* is a person being treated unfairly? *Why* is a person poor?

Answering these questions means examining how the UCC, its members, and its nation are complicit with injustice. It requires a willingness to change structures, actions, and thinking in alignment with Jesus the righteous. It means repenting of our systemic sinfulness.

One example of this is found in the United Church of Christ's effort to change the baseball team name of the Cleveland Indians. While not a popular struggle with loyal Cleveland fans, it is an attempt to find a way not to patronize or denigrate a people. It is right to demand self-examination every time the "Tomahawk Chop" is invoked at sports events.

Another example is found in the movement to provide Fair Trade Coffee in our local congregations. Products that are sustainably grown are important for our earth. Providing a fair wage for a product helps entire communities care for themselves.

Still another example is a 1959 federal court ruling that the airwaves are public and not private property. That decision resulted from the efforts of Everett Parker of the UCC's Office of Communications. He organized churches to confront the Southern television stations' media blackout of the civil rights movement.

Each of these examples points to the issue of stewardship. How do we care for God's gifts of one another and of the earth? How do we respond with gratitude to God for the great blessings in our lives?

Stewardship is about more than putting an envelope in a Sunday offering plate. It is about recognizing that when we care for our bodies, we honor God. When we help one another, we honor

God. When we engage our resources for the goodwill of our families, communities, nation, and world, we honor God. When we work for justice on behalf of those with no voice, God is honored. When we work for peace and reconciliation, God is honored.

This stewardship context is suggested by an ancient Chinese proverb in which one is encouraged to live each day as if it were one's last and as if one will live a thousand years. In other words, our actions must be weighed against abundance and scarcity. If this is the last day, what actions must be taken? If we look ahead a thousand years, what must we do today to ensure that future? The United Church of Christ seeks to take these questions of stewardship seriously.

COREM

Are you racking your brain trying to remember where you have heard COREM before? Was it a Bible story? A Jewish festival? Just exactly where did you hear of COREM?

The Council of Racial Ethnic Minorities (COREM) was convened in 1983. It was then, through the inspired efforts of Héctor López, that racial ethnic interest groups within the UCC met to seek out a new structure. López was able to persuade the leadership of the Council for Hispanic Ministries (CHM), the Council for American Indian Ministries (CAIM), the Pacific Islander and Asian American Ministry (PAAM), United Black Christians (UBC) and Ministers for Racial and Social Justice (MRSJ), to work together. Each of these ministries would continue their vital work in the denomination, but together they would have a more effective presence in the UCC with a seat on the Executive Council and inclusion in General Synod and in the instrumentalities of the denomination.

The work of COREM is not simple or easy, but it is necessary. It is one way for the United Church of Christ to be united and uniting, as it seeks to be. The witness and work of COREM pushes the denomination to more sensitive inclusion and justice.

GIVE ME AN "E"

What is evangelism? Why has it become known as the "E" word in the United Church of Christ?

Evangelism comes from the Greek word *evangel,* or "good news." Evangelism is spreading the good news about the Good News, Jesus Christ. That means that every time one tells how God is working in one's life, one is proclaiming that news as an evangelist.

There is among some people a reticence to belong to a church that describes itself as evangelical. Across our nation, evangelical is used to describe those with a fundamentalist faith who interpret the Bible literally and inerrantly. These evangelicals concern themselves with the state of a person's soul and ask, "Have you been saved?"

Instead, the United Church of Christ embraces an evangelism that shares the good news of how God is working in our lives, in our churches, in our denomination, and in the world. In an address by UCC president John Thomas, one can hear the proclamation of the good news contrasted with what he calls "respectable religion" (see the following page). He challenges the denomination and individual congregations and members to go outside of their church walls, and invite the community in, sharing the great good news of Jesus with others.

But that invitation makes some people squirm. Does that mean that we must convert all persons to accept Jesus Christ as Savior? What does that mean about ecumenism and interfaith relationships? The UCC is respectful of other expressions of Christianity and of other religions. At the same time, the UCC is aware of the need to share the good news with those who have not found a spiritual home.

FROM RESPECTABLE RELIGION TO EVANGELICAL FAITH

From the Annual Meeting of the Southeast Conference of the United Church of Christ, June 2007, by John H. Thomas, General Minister and President, United Church of Christ.

Respectable religion is preoccupied with the people already in the church, caring only for ourselves as if we were one great chaplaincy to each other.

Evangelical faith is deeply attentive to those outside the church, to the spiritually homeless yearning for a relationship with Jesus and with the community of Christ's people.

Respectable religion fears transgressing the rules. It guards the door and is always "well-behaved."

Evangelical faith knows that the love of God and the love of neighbor ultimately trump the authority of both the canons and the clerics and will not stand for bouncers or ejector seats in our churches.

Respectable religion is afflicted with terminal politeness. It will never risk offending, even with the truth.

Evangelical faith rises up with outrage on behalf of the poor and oppressed and violated in our world who are left out, left alone, left behind.

Respectable religion blesses the culture and seeks to protect its own privileged place in the world.

Evangelical faith challenges the culture and risks the embrace of those at the margins.

Respectable religion seeks a congenial place where cross and flag can easily cohabit to claim our dual allegiance.

Evangelical faith calls into question every parochial idolatry and places us under the sole and sovereign claim of our Lord.

Respectable religion wants at all cost to avoid standing out; its cry is "please don't make me feel embarrassed."

Evangelical faith is prepared to be odd, a peculiar salt and leaven in the world.

Respectable religion prays for the victims of war and for those in harm's way.

Evangelical faith does this, but also challenges the arrogance and deception of those who lead us to war.

Respectable religion treats the church's Book as a shrine to be worshiped, a talisman to be carried, an armor for protection.

Evangelical faith opens the Book to hear the surprising, confounding voice of the still-speaking God.

Respectable religion views the offering as at best a "necessary evil," a time to give "just enough." It finds talk about money intrusive and offensive.

Evangelical faith sees the offering as an act of gratitude and joy, a time for extravagance and dance!

Respectable religion is an older brother ever grumpy that grace abounds for those deemed undeserving.

Evangelical faith is a waiting mother or father eager to embrace the one returning from a far country.

Respectable religion is always serious, sober, and somber.

Evangelical faith plays, teases, pokes fun, provokes us toward joy!

KIDDING?

We've all experienced something like this. The children are called forward for the children's sermon. The pastor describes something that eats berries and seeds, that drinks water, that has beautiful colors, and flies. The pastor asks the children what is being described, and a young one says, "It sounds like a bird, but I know the answer is Jesus!"

That is an example of a typical involvement of children in worship. We sort of want the children there. That is, when they're quiet and well behaved. We even say that children are the future of our church. But that's really goofy thinking. Children are already part of the church. They are gifts to all of us from a loving God. They challenge our assumptions, surprise us with wisdom, stun us with sensitivity, and call forth our caring not only for them but for all who share the earth.

They belong in worship, in Sunday School, in children's choirs, in ministries of outreach, and at church dinners. Congregations that affirm the presence of children will see that they have children's bulletins and activity bags to help them find their own ways to participate in the worship experience. They can serve as acolytes, greeters, and ushers. They can design and make banners for the sanctuary. They can walk in a Church World Service CROP Walk to raise money and awareness for hungry people.

Yet it isn't just a question of what children are capable of. They also need to be in worship. They need to be in worship to see what happens there, to observe baptisms and participate in them, to share Holy Communion. They need to become comfortable with praising God, to understand how and why we pray, to become familiar with the Lord's Prayer, with hymns, and songs.

Each congregation decides how to include its children. At what age is Holy Communion celebrated with children? Do the children attend the entire worship service or simply the part before or after Sunday School?

Should there be a worship service each year led by children? Is that enough? Are there parents on your worship planning committee? Are there children who can help make some of the worship decisions?

And let us not forget our youth. It is appropriate and helpful to have youthful vision and leadership in congregational structures. Think of youth not just as potential worship leaders for Youth Sundays or as a treasurer of leaf-rakers or window washers. Think of youth when you are slating church boards.

Our worship communities will be richer for the inclusion of our children and youth. All "kidding" aside.

WHAT'S AN ACTIVITY BAG?

An activity bag is a colorful bag that a child can pick up on her or his way into the sanctuary when it is time for worship. It may include:

A picture or two to color	A cloth book
A few crayons	A pad of paper
A puppet	

It usually does not include these things:

A whistle	Lollipops with short sticks
A glue stick	Marbles
A rubber duck	

GENERALLY SPEAKING

Every two years, according to the Constitution of the United Church of Christ, the denomination is to gather together to address issues of importance to the national church and to our world. In an effort to include the broadest participation possible the location of General Synod is moved around the country.

Representatives from across the church are sent to these meetings. Each of the denomination's conferences sends delegates who have been elected to serve in this capacity. Representatives from a great diversity of working ministries and committees also come to these meetings. National staff and church officers are also in attendance, as are many visitors.

Exciting and inspiring worship, workshops, resolution and pronouncement discussions, and displays on ministries from across the breadth of the church and from its ecumenical partners and affiliated ministries highlight General Synod. Attendees receive reports, join in enthusiastic singing, and hear amazing stories from people in the denomination. General Synod offers opportunities to participate in events like blood drives and other mission events benefiting the host community.

It is an awesome time. Many describe these gatherings as life-changing. Happily, each General Synod also gathers a significant number of youth from our denomination. They participate in their own activities and join in some of the General Synod happenings as well.

One common feature of the UCC General Synods is the wonderful variety and number of cookies that are offered to delegates and visitors. In Hartford, Connecticut, site of the 2007

General Synod, 216,000 cookies were available. The varieties were astonishing: wheat-free, nut-free, sugar-free, dairy-free, peanut-free, broccoli-free. Okay, all the cookies, as far as we know, were broccoli-free. At the end of the Synod, many homeless persons from the area were given dozens of cookies from the event. They, too, participated in the UCC's greatest cookie event ever, bar none!

HYMN FOR SYNODICAL HALLWAYS
(sung to "Blessed Assurance")

God is still speaking, so let me say
You're welcome in my church: straight folks or gay.
Sponge Bob is welcome. Tinkie Wink, too.
We are a family — red states or blue.
God is still speaking, oh what relief
That God's still unfolding our every belief.

We are unfinished, seeking the way,
Hoping to live in light every day.
Taking positions, making a stand,
Striving for justice throughout the land.
Livable wages, safe water for all,
Responsible living that is our call.

God is still speaking, all our hearts soar.
Together, united, we'll stand with the poor.
Learning to listen, daring to speak,
Where one heart is hurting, all hearts are weak.

ROLLIN' IN THE DOUGH

Editor's Note: This recipe is offered as a public service and as a "prayer request" for future General Synods.

Ingredients:

2¼ cup flour	¾ cup sugar
1 tsp. baking soda	¾ cup brown sugar, packed
½ tsp. salt	1 tsp. vanilla
1 cup butter	2 eggs
1 cup vegetable shortening	1¾ cups chocolate chips

PREHEAT oven to 375 degrees

MELT butter and shortening. Add sugars and vanilla. Cool.

MIX flour, baking soda, and salt.

ADD eggs to cooled butter/shortening/sugar mixture. Beat well.

GRADUALLY add flour mixture.

STIR in chocolate chips.

DROP by rounded spoon on ungreased cookie sheets.

BAKE for 9 to 11 minutes.

COOL on wire racks.

(Note: 1 cup of nuts may be added if desired.)

SIX

Looking at Our Witness

CHALLENGED TO WALK THE WALK

Centrifugal force — the force impelling a thing (or person) outward from the center — was a central characteristic of Jesus' ministry. At the beginning, on a visit to his hometown synagogue in Nazareth, Jesus was handed the scroll of Isaiah to read. He chose segments from 61:1–2 and 58:6, and then spoke about how God's love and compassion extended outward to include foreigners. After this unwelcome bit of biblical exegesis he was nearly lynched by the congregation. (You will find this story in Luke 4:16–30.)

At the end of his earthly sojourn, Jesus commissioned his disciples to make disciples of all nations (Matt. 28:19–20). This commission to go outward was quoted again in Acts 1:8, "You will be my witnesses in Jerusalem, in all Judea and Samaria, and to the ends of the earth."

In the early 1800s our forebears felt this centrifugal force quite strongly (as did the forebears of other denominational groups). They felt called to move out across the earth to bring light to all the dark places, to Christianize and civilize the heathen. The goal as they saw it was to enable converts to become English-proficient in language, civilized in habits, and Christian in religion. Basic mission work in this early period included evangelism and church planting, education, literacy, technical training, and health care.

Missionaries in these early days traveled out on merchant boats primarily to lands that were European colonies or being opened to European and U.S. trade (much as Paul did when he visited cities that were important economic centers in the Roman Empire). As our forebear missionaries began to live among the people to be evangelized, however, they came to see the people around them not as objects but as subjects, brothers and sisters in God's family.

A striking example of this took place in the mission work of our forebears as they moved out into the Judeas and Samarias of their day. One of their mission fields was among the Cherokee Indians in the southeastern part of our country — work that was sponsored at that time by the American Board of Commissioners for Foreign Missions.

Mission centers were established in what is now Chattanooga, Tennessee, and New Echota, Georgia. Our forebears, especially through the efforts of Rev. Samuel A. Worcester and Dr. Elizur Butler, worked with Sequoyah and other Cherokee leaders to bring into existence a written Cherokee language, a constitution, schools, and their own newspaper.

Unfortunately, gold was discovered on Cherokee land, and the state of Georgia sought to evict the Cherokees from the territory where treaties had given them possession as a sovereign nation. Our forebears joined the Cherokees in fighting this effort, taking the case to the Supreme Court, which supported the Indians in its verdict. This verdict, however, was ignored by the state of

Georgia and President Andrew Jackson. Georgia then passed a law prohibiting white men from entering Indian country without a license from the state. Eleven missionaries were arrested for violating the law. Nine accepted pardons, promising not to violate the law again, but Worcester and Butler refused to obey the law and were sentenced to four years of hard labor in the state penitentiary. This ruling was then reversed by the Supreme Court.

In 1830, Congress, pushed by President Jackson, passed the Indian Removal Act. A small unauthorized group of Cherokees agreed on behalf of all the Cherokees to a new treaty with Washington to sell their eastern lands for $5 million and to move beyond the Mississippi River to Indian Territory. President Martin Van Buren then ordered the implementation of the treaty in 1838. Over twenty thousand Cherokees were rounded up and forced by U.S. soldiers to migrate by river and by land. On the land route, known as "The Trail Where They Cried," or "The Trail of Tears," over four thousand Cherokees lost their lives because of illness, poor traveling conditions, and winter cold.

Rev. Worcester went on to Oklahoma to meet the Cherokees there, but Dr. Butler accompanied them on the trail, walking the walk with them.

"CROSSING" THE GLOBE

In the early days of foreign missions, the Gospel's centrifugal force took our forebears to such areas as the Holy Land, Iraq, Syria, Turkey, India, South Africa, Rhodesia, Japan, the Philippines, the Sandwich Islands (Hawaii), Micronesia, China, and Honduras. Over the years, the Christianizing and civilizing mission became more holistic, collegial, and cognizant of mutual relationships — a project in sharing the good news in life, word, and service. Our UCC ancestors founded churches, hospitals, secondary schools, colleges, seminaries, as well as literacy, leadership development, community, and economic development programs. They were also heavily involved in refugee assistance and emergency relief programs.

In all of these programs there was a heavy commitment to working ecumenically in each country and to supporting the national church councils as well as the work of the World Council of Churches. There was also a basic assumption: that the mission work would eventually be taken over and led by nationals rather than by foreigners.

All through this process, a basic perspective came to be acknowledged: the very nature of God is missionary and sending. The church, as a community of God's followers, becomes an instrument of God rather than the proprietor of the action. The church does not *have* a mission; it *is* mission. Along with this was a growing awareness, also, that economic liberation and reconciliation are important facets of mission.

The following picture from 1970 indicates the heavy investment of personnel during this period:

- Pacific Region:123 missionaries in 7 countries (most in Japan, the Philippines, and Micronesia).

- Africa Region:103 missionaries in 15 countries (most in South Africa, Rhodesia, Ghana, and Zambia).

- Near East Region: 89 missionaries in 2 countries (most in Turkey).

- Southern Asia Region: 56 missionaries in 2 countries (most in India).

- Latin America Region: 30 missionaries in 6 countries (most in Honduras).

- Europe Region: 9 missionaries in 8 countries (most in Greece, France, Germany, and Italy).

Over the years, additional mission emphases and perspectives have been added to the basic ones mentioned above. Through our global ministries we are supporting the following important kinds of programs:

* evangelization and new church development
* the development and strengthening of existing churches
* leadership development
* promotion of health and wholeness
* sustainable economic and community development
* advocacy for peace and justice
* interfaith dialogue
* reconciliation of ethnic and national tensions
* partners expressing a Christian witness in a secular society
* feeding hungry people
* combating human rights abuses

Today in this new era of collegial mission, we have 57 fully supported missionaries living in 29 countries. Thirty percent of the staff are from racial/ethnic minority constituencies.

* Africa: 14 missionaries in 6 countries
* East Asia and the Pacific: 13 missionaries in 5 countries
* Middle East and Europe: 13 missionaries in 6 countries
* Southern Asia: 9 missionaries in 6 countries
* Latin America and the Caribbean: 8 missionaries in 6 countries

The current mission statement of our UCC Global Ministries expresses both the historical and contemporary understanding of our mission calling:

> We commit ourselves to a shared life in Christ and to an ecumenical global sharing of resources and prophetic vision of a just and peaceful world order, joining with God's concern for the poor and oppressed. This commitment will be

reflected in common decision-making for mission program which will visibly witness to the oneness of mission in and through the Church of Jesus Christ.

And so Christians in all nations meet beneath the cross and join together to share a common mission: Jesus' passionate concern for the poor, captive, blind, and oppressed (Luke 4:18–19).

MISSION IMPROBABLE

Increasing numbers of Christians are beginning to see the United States as one of the most important mission fields in the world. Our domestic and foreign policy, our use of the world's resources, our values and goals, our sense of hubris all have a direct impact upon the world. What we say and do affects the rest of the world, but we are often isolated from what the rest of the world says and does.

Living in the metropolitan center of a world empire, we are in the same kind of bubble the master and mistress of a slave plantation lived in, not knowing about the real lives and thoughts of their slaves. News from the rest of the world is filtered through corporate media. When problems develop in the rest of the world, we build walls to keep the problems out or try to find military solutions. And now we are building drone aircraft and robot landcraft that we can direct from the United States for use around the world to prevent any vulnerability to enemy opposition.

It is hard to live lives of empathy, compassion, and solidarity in such a world. In the past the United Church of Christ has invited church representatives from other countries to serve as "missioners" in our country, working with conference staffs, seminary faculties, and national boards and ministries. This "reverse" or "two-way" mission has enriched the life of the UCC and needs to be implemented even further in a time such as this.

The most important questions of our faith today need to be discussed by Christians meeting together across national and ethnic barriers. The dynamism of the early missionary movement came out of the Pentecostal experience of believers from many nations coming together to talk, eat, and worship together — and to share their possessions and wealth with any as had need (Acts 2:5–13, 43–47).

One of the important questions for international discussion today is a basic one: What exactly is the good news we proclaim? Peter Gomes raises this question in the title of one of his books: *The Scandalous Gospel of Jesus: What's So Good about the Good News?* When missionaries Pliny Fiske and Levi Parsons went to Palestine in 1819, they asked two important questions relating to goodness: "What good can be done?" and "By what means?" These are crucial questions for us today, not only for the church but also for our nation in its domestic and foreign relations.

Another important question relating to goodness has to do with "the common good" — the idea that there is a good to which all members of a society (or God's human family) should have access, and for whose enjoyment no one should be excluded. Such a good is to be shared and beneficial to all.

This is a critical moral issue confronting our own nation — a land of private affluence and public poverty. As Jonathan Rowe has written,

> The commons is a kind of counterpoise to the market. It provides stability and sustenance rather than restless appetite and craving. It connects to the "we" side of human nature as opposed to the market's unrelenting "me." The concept includes anything not owned but shared in common.... If one thing sums up commons-based economic policy, it is community ... the desire to connect with others rather than to stand apart. This side is increasingly repressed in America today.[1]

---

1. Jonathan Rowe, "The Demand for the Common Good," *www.yesmagazine.com/article.asp?ID=868.*

The concept of "the common good" is important, also, in a world context. We are called as Christians to be global citizens and to be agents of transformation in the world.

Mission improbable — or mission imperative? Our missionary God continues to challenge us.

THE UCC APOLOGIZES TO HAWAII

In 1993, UCC president Paul Sherry delivered an apology to the people of Hawaii. It was an apology asked for by some native Hawaiians and their UCC supporters who brought a resolution supporting Native Hawaiian sovereignty to the Hawaii Conference Annual Meeting and then to General Synod in 1993. It acknowledged the benefits that Euro-Americans received when their ancestors participated in the cultural genocide of the people of Hawaii. It admitted that some of our UCC forebears participated in the illegal overthrow of the Hawaiian monarchy.

Although the apology was heard by thousands of native Hawaiians, the Hawaii Conference was divided in its response, deciding to receive the president and not accept the apology. Those working for Hawaii's sovereignty insisted that redress become part of the UCC apology. Eventually this was done through grants from the Hawaii Conference and also from the United Church Boards for Home and World Ministries.

Is this apology the start of redress for others our church forebears wronged? What is the responsibility for those generations that have followed, and benefited, from such injustice? Why should peoples who have been historically mistreated continue to suffer? These are only a few questions that the United Church of Christ continues to probe.

RESOLUTIONS: NOT JUST FOR TVs

When the United Church of Christ gathers every two years as a General Synod, it takes upon itself the task of addressing resolutions. These resolutions, when adopted, speak to the church. Though hardly a comprehensive list, topics that General Synod has addressed include:

Justice and peace resolutions for the church

Declaring the UCC to be an Anti-racism church

Declaring the UCC to be a Just Peace Church

Offering a Christian response to genetic advances

Offering an alternative voice to Christian Zionism

Supporting those who refuse to pay taxes for military preparations

Confessing of the UCC's forebears' participation in the establishment of Indian boarding schools

Declaring the UCC to be a Fair Trade denomination

Justice and peace resolutions for the United States

Adopting Jubilee for Justice for the rural United States

Addressing immigration justice and reform

Responding to AIDS discrimination

Demanding access to excellence in public schools

Studying reparations for slavery

Demanding the closing of the U.S. Army School of the Americas

Demanding campaign finance reform

Addressing the cloning of mammalian species

Working for a compassionate response to substance abuse

Supporting the Coalition of Immokalee Workers boycott of Taco Bell

Supporting religious freedom for Hawaiian prisoners

Supporting federally funded research on embryonic stem cells

Acting in faithful accompaniment of farm workers

Urging welfare reform

Justice and peace resolutions for the world

Working for justice for the Micronesian Islands

Urging withdrawal of U.S. bases from Okinawa

Urging withdrawal of the U.S. Navy from Vieques, Puerto Rico

Working for more humane direction for economic globalization

Declaring solidarity with the persecuted in the Philippines

Addressing climate change

Affirming partnership with the Council of Churches in Cuba

Demanding democracy and human rights in Nigeria

Opposing female genital mutilation

Addressing conflict diamonds in Sierra Leone

Supporting the investigation into human rights violations in the Philippines

Demanding peace and reconciliation in the Korean Peninsula

Supporting a comprehensive ban on landmines

Supporting a global nonviolent peace force

Promoting peace in the Sudan

Supporting the International Criminal Court

To date, the UCC has adopted twenty-seven resolutions in support of gay men, lesbians, bisexual, and transgender persons. Its witness is unparalleled in mainline Christian denominations.

WON'T YOU LET ME BE YOUR SERVANT?

We are pilgrims on a journey, we are travelers on the road,
We are here to help each other go the mile and bear the load.

— "Won't You Let Me Be Your Servant?"
Hymn #539 from *The New Century Hymnal*

As UCC members and others go through the various stages of life, there is a UCC agency that has a special concern: that everyone on this journey have the opportunity, as much as possible, to live life to the fullest. The UCC **Council for Health and Human Service Ministries** (CHHSM) has this important mission and brings some 360 organizations and programs together to help support and advance their ministries of healing and service.

Indicative of the fact that our population is living longer, **services to the aging** represent the largest number of programs and facilities: 191. These include apartments, residences, manors, retirement centers, and villages offering various kinds of programs and special health care. Two long-established communities — Uplands Retirement Village in Pleasant Hill, Tennessee, and Pilgrim Place in Claremont, California — each offer a caring environment for over 350 retirees. An indication that these specialized environments seek to add life to one's years as well as years to one's life is the Uplands invitation appearing in the *United Church News:* "Believers in peace and justice never retire.... They just move to Uplands!"

Services to children, youth, and families comprise the second largest segment of programs: 31. These include a wide variety of facilities and programs: children's homes, neighborhood houses, community centers, inner city missions, and family services.

Neighborhood houses in many inner cities are helping the working class and immigrant population address the issues of inadequate housing, lack of medical attention, and poor education for their children. The website of Neighborhood Houses in St. Louis, *www.neighborhoodhouses.org* gives a good introduction to this kind of challenging ministry.

One unusual outreach program is the Back Bay Mission established by the Evangelical Church in 1922 to address the needs of poor "fisher folk" living in deplorable conditions along the Back Bay of Biloxi, Mississippi. After Hurricane Katrina struck in August 2005, Back Bay Mission lost its habitable facilities. With the help of two donated trailers, the mission continued its vital work of education, legal aid, health care, feeding programs, early childhood development, family counseling, housing, and domestic violence.

Services to persons with developmental disabilities make up the third segment of programs: 20. These include homes and apartments.

Primary and acute health care services make up the fourth segment of facilities and programs: 16. These include hospitals, medical centers, and parish nurse ministries.

For more information, check out the CHHSM website at *www.chhsm.org.*

The **Outdoor Ministries Association** (OMA) of the United Church of Christ, in addition to CHHSM, is another agency concerned about young travelers along the road of life. Through

OMA, persons responsible for outdoor ministries in the UCC, in more than sixty UCC camp, conference, and retreat programs across the country, work together to meet the needs and find common solutions in the area of outdoor ministry. Their website is *www.oma-ucc.org.*

PASSING THE BUCK

OCWM, Our Church's Wider Mission, is the name for the fund that supports conferences, national settings, and UCC-related institutions. In some local congregations, dedicated offerings and per capita dues are collected for OCWM support. Many local congregations collect four special offerings during the calendar year: One Great Hour of Sharing, Strengthen the Church, Neighbors in Need, and the Christmas Fund. These four offerings are promoted through the national church offices as directed by the General Synod.

One Great Hour of Sharing is generally received on the fourth Sunday in Lent. This offering provides support for our partners in over seventy countries. By funding development projects and responding to disasters like war, famine, tsunamis, and earthquakes, the UCC helps to restore hope and dignity to populations that are displaced and suffering. In our denomination the ministries that oversee these areas are Wider Church Ministries and Global Sharing of Resources.

Strengthen the Church is received on Pentecost Sunday. This offering supports leadership development and church growth in both the conferences and national offices of Local Church Ministries. As of 2008 some funds of this offering will be dedicated to the "God is still speaking" initiative.

Neighbors in Need is received on World Communion Sunday which is celebrated the first Sunday of October. This offering supports ministries of justice and compassion throughout the United States and Puerto Rico, through the efforts of the Council for American Indian Ministries (CAIM) and by the national offices of Justice and Witness Ministries.

The Christmas Fund is received on the Sunday before Christmas. Its funds are distributed by the Pension Boards to retired and active ministers, their surviving spouses, and children with difficult financial circumstances.

THIS SHOULD MAKE YOU INTERESTED

When UCC churches or members invest in the Cornerstone Fund, they receive a competitive rate of interest for their investment. In turn the Fund uses the principal invested to loan congregations and other organizations related to the UCC the money needed for purchasing land or remodeling or repairing their facilities. Such capital improvements can be difficult for congregations, but thanks to the Cornerstone Fund, created in 1995, necessary monies can be made available. This is a creative way to expand the stewardship of congregations, organizations, and individuals. For more information, call 888-822-3863.

ARE WE FULL YET?

The United Church of Christ hopes to be not only a united church but also a uniting church, seeking to heal the divisions within the Body of Christ. It was Jesus' hope, expressed in the Gospel of John (John 17:21), that is ever at the forefront of our efforts to connect with our Christian sisters and brothers and with interfaith communities as well.

Connecting with other Christian traditions helps us learn more about their spiritual practices and enlightens our own practices and history as well. Working together with ecumenical partners offers us the opportunity to serve the world more effectively.

Directed by General Synod, our ecumenical commitment in part is expressed through the work of the National Council of Churches and the World Council of Churches.

The National Council of Churches plays a key ecumenical role in our nation, bringing together thirty-three churches and a hundred thousand local congregations. Its Statement of Faith reads as follows: "The National Council of Churches is a community of Christian communions, which, in response to the gospel as revealed in the Scriptures, confess Jesus Christ, the incarnate Word of God, as Savior and Lord. These communions covenant with one another to manifest ever more fully the unity of the Church. Relying upon the transforming power of the Holy Spirit, the communions come together as the Council in common mission, serving in all creation to the glory of God. . . .

"As they gather in the Council, the member communions **grow** in understanding of each other's tradition. They work to identify and fully **claim** those areas of belief they hold in common; they **celebrate** the diverse and unique gifts that each church brings to ecumenical life; and together they **study** those issues that divide the churches. And they **cooperate** in many joint programs of education, adovacy, and service that address critically important needs and that witness to our common faith in Jesus Christ."

The National Council of Churches provided for the translation process that produced the Revised Standard Version and the New Revised Standard Version of the Bible; it also collects and publishes the annual *Yearbook of American and Canadian Churches*. Its offices are located in New York City.

Rev. Dr. Michael Kinnamon, a Christian Church (Disciples of Christ) clergyman, educator, and ecumenical leader, was unanimously elected to the office General Secretary of the National Council of Churches in November 2007. Previous to that, he had served for seven years as the Allen and Dottie Miller Professor of Mission, Peace and Ecumenical Studies at the UCC Eden Theological Seminary in Webster Groves, Missouri.

The World Council of Churches brings together 349 churches, denominations, and church fellowships in more than 110 countries and territories throughout the world. "As members of this fellowship, WCC member churches are called to the goal of visible unity in one faith and one eucharistic fellowship; promote their common witness in work for mission and evangelism; engage in Christian service by serving human need, breaking down barriers between people, seeking justice and peace, and upholding the integrity of creation; and foster renewal in unity, worship, mission, and service."

The WCC has six programs:

1. The WCC and the ecumenical movement in the twenty-first century

2. Unity, mission, evangelism, and spirituality

3. Public witness: addressing power, affirming peace

4. Justice, Diakonia, and Responsibility for Creation

5. Education and ecumenical formation

6. Inter-religious dialogue and cooperation

Its main offices are in Geneva, Switzerland, with a U.S. office in New York City.

Around our denomination are countless examples of interfaith dialogue and service projects. In this country, UCC members walk with Muslim and Buddhist brothers and sisters to raise money for the hungry through Church World Service's CROP Hunger Walks. Christian/Islamic dialogues explore differences and similarities of our faiths and open us to the blessings of knowing our human family. Abroad, our missionaries are significantly involved in interfaith relationships.

Finally, the UCC is working to establish full communion with the separated branches of the Body of Christ.[2] We enjoy a relationship with the Christian Church (Disciples of Christ). Some UCC churches are served by Disciples' pastors and UCC pastors can be called to serve Disciples' churches. We celebrate the Formula of Agreement, a covenant with the Evangelical Lutheran Church in America, Presbyterian Church (USA), and the Reformed Church in America. Finally, Churches United in Christ (CUIC) is working to establish full communion among nine Protestant and Anglican churches in the United States. If CUIC is successful, African American and European American churches will enjoy full communion for the first time in history.

FROM WELLS TO BLANKETS, WE'VE GOT YOU COVERED

Our world has been in continuous war for decades. Those wars have poisoned air, water, food supplies, and soil. They have created a refugee crisis beyond comprehension. They have disrupted and displaced whole families and fragments of them. They have fed a spiraling cycle of violence that has no end in sight.

When our world is not addressing the cost and casualties of war, it is struggling with environmental crises: lands contaminated by toxic waste dumps, death and destruction following tsunamis, earthquakes, and famines.

---

2. Full communion means that churches recognize each others' sacraments and provide for the orderly transfer of ministers from one denomination to another.

How can we respond to all of the world's needs without sinking into utter despair? One way is to help each other address these needs. That means congregations and communities all across the nation coming together to make a difference in the lives of those who are suffering. It means bringing together people of all faiths and nations to harness the possibilities for repair, reconstruction, reforestation, and the like.

That's why the United Church of Christ partners with Church World Service. It is the agency that helps us with disaster relief, refugee resettlement, and long-term self-help development assistance. Through CWS, our efforts help more than eighty countries around the world. Wells are dug, seeds planted, shelters built, and food and water resources shared. Education and literacy programs are also provided.

Church World Service can do these things on our behalf and with us because they themselves partner not only with the United Church of Christ but also thirty-four other denominations. CWS extends the reach of our One Great Hour of Sharing and our Neighbors in Need offerings.

SEVEN

Looking to the Future

PRAISE THE LORD
WITH CLANGING SYMBOLS (Ps. 150:5)

We began this handbook taking a look at the three symbols in the UCC's founding logo — the cross, crown, and orb. As we have come to understand the significance of a fourth symbol — the comma — both for the UCC's faith journey and for the journey of our spiritual ancestors in their struggle to be receptive and faithful to a still-speaking God, we have included that as an important one, too.

It is appropriate to call our experience with this still-speaking God a journey and not a destination. Although there are basic verities and truths we claim, we always encounter surprises along the way — new understandings, new stretchings, new horizons.

As we come to a close, we offer a parting look at these four, both in terms of the past and what they may mean for us in the future.

THE FOUR SYMBOLS IN JESUS' TIME

1. Orb

In Jesus' time and place people thought that the earth was flat and at the center of the universe. They did not have much idea of any world beyond the Mediterranean region that at that time was part of the Roman Empire. Rome's military, political, economic, and ideological power was the main "fact of life" in each country. As John Dominic Crossan has written in his book *God and Empire*, "Rome spoke of itself in transcendental terms as an empire divinely mandated to rule without limits of time or place. It did not simply proclaim dominion around the Mediterranean Sea. It announced world conquest, global rule, and eternal sovereignty."[1]

The imperial theology at the heart of this Pax Romana was based on Rome's divine mission in the world, on the worship of the appropriate gods, and on the divinity of the emperor, whose titles were God, Son of God, Lord, Redeemer, Liberator, and Savior of the World. Even Caesar's coins carried the inscription "Son of God."

The dark underside of this "Roman Peace" was its hierarchical relationships, concentration of wealth, widespread poverty, violence, oppression, and continual warfare.

---

1. John Dominic Crossan, *God and Empire: Jesus against Rome, Then, and Now* (San Francisco: HarperSanFrancisco, 2007), 15.

This Roman context was an important fact of life in Jesus' environment. The close collaboration between Rome and Herod the Great, the Jewish king who had been appointed by Rome, was evident in several huge construction projects. He created a new port in Caesarea, constructed three new temples to the emperor Augustus, and expanded the Gentile plaza of the Jerusalem Temple to the size of five football fields.

Jesus grew up in Nazareth, about four miles from Sepphoris, the Roman-controlled capital of Galilee, and was well aware of the harmful impact of Rome's colonial rule in his country. The Roman power structure worked closely with a collaborating Jewish power structure in Jerusalem — with the king in the palace and chief priests in the Temple.

2. Cross

When Jesus began his ministry, he announced that the realm of God was at hand — a new ordering of life in which God and not Caesar or Herod would be on the throne. It would be a new kind of community in which the sick were healed, the poor welcomed, and possessions shared. A different value system would begin. The common people heard this as good news, but the Roman and Jewish officials took this as a direct threat to their peace and order.

The double demonstration during Jesus' last week in Jerusalem — the anti-imperial entry into the city and the symbolic destruction of the Temple — sealed his fate. Jesus was nailed to a cross — the primary instrument of terror and capital punishment used by Rome throughout its empire for troublemakers. Alternative kings and kingdoms were not to be tolerated. A warning sign for any with alternative thoughts was placed above him, "This is Jesus, the King of the Jews."

3. Crown

On Easter morning the disciples had a transforming experience. They encountered an empty tomb, a risen Presence, and understood this new development as God's veto of the imperial verdict.

From then on, they and other followers were bold to make treasonous claims: It was Jesus, not Caesar, who was divinely conceived. It was God's peace and not Caesar's that was announced by angels, and it was a Savior who was not Caesar who was welcomed by them and by shepherds. Even wise men from the East had shown up asking a treasonous question that greatly disturbed Herod, "Where is the child who has been born king of the Jews?" This, then, is why Mark began his story with such a bold, treasonous statement, "The beginning of the good news of Jesus Christ, the Son of God."

Here was a new kind of Lord or Sovereign — one who continued to invite us into a new kind of kingdom or realm. Some called it a new kind of empire; others, a new kind of commonwealth or kingdom. These terms were all ways of describing a new kind of relationship to each other and to a still-speaking God.

4. Comma

Jesus, through his words and actions, proclaimed an energizing truth that God was still speaking. Many times he said, "You have heard it said of old... but I say to you...." His deeds of healing, forgiving, and welcoming constantly astonished those around him. And many felt threatened.

The Jewish and Roman establishment sought to place periods all through Jesus' life and especially at the end. But God placed commas instead. There was still more to come. That is why Mark stated in his Gospel introduction that it was the *beginning* of the good news. The acts of the apostles were still to follow, even to this very day!

THE FOUR SYMBOLS IN OUR TIME

1. Orb

We now have quite a different view of our earth than in Jesus' time: a lovely blue and white planet in space (in a photo taken from the moon), circling around our sun in a universe full of stars and galaxies. And we now have much more information about this planet we live on.

We know that our spiritual ancestors had it right: that we stand on ground that is holy, and that we are called to be careful and loving caretakers of this earthly home of ours. And yet we humans continue to poison this nest of ours. We are coming to realize that global warming is a theological as well as an environmental issue and that the survival of all life on this planet is now at risk. Sin, repentance, atonement, being born again (or "from above," as the Bible actually puts it), restitution, and Jubilee all have special meaning today in light of this planetary disobedience.

And we now know that the imperial context of Jesus' time is not a thing of the past. Only now we find ourselves in a different location. We in the United States do not live in a colony of an empire as Jesus did, but in Rome itself — in the headquarters of the Pax Americana, the greatest empire in the history of the world. It is an empire maintained by 2,639 permanent military bases in the United States and its territories, and by 737 permanent foreign bases.

It is an empire built on a growing divide between the rich and the poor, the well-fed and the hungry, and the extraction of the world's resources for the benefit of those in the headquarters. It is built on the value of individualism rather than community, on market value rather than justice, and maintained through the utilization of violence and war on behalf of "peace and order" and the security and well-being of those who live in the imperial headquarters. Here sin, repentance, atonement, being born again, restitution, and Jubilee also have special meaning in light of this planetary arrogance.

2. Cross

This Roman instrument of capital punishment has become our primary Christian symbol. Roman Catholic churches prefer to use a crucifix — a cross with Jesus' body fastened to it. Most Protestant churches, however, prefer an empty, resurrection cross. A stained-glass window in the chapel of Eden Theological Seminary has an interesting perspective on this: It shows a risen Jesus holding the cross rather than being held by it.

These two versions also point to different interpretations of the meaning of "passion." The crucifix suggests that the passion of Christ referred to his last hours of suffering on the cross. The empty cross, in contrast, suggests that the passion of Christ was what he was passionate about in his life — about healing, including, welcoming, and transforming.

While the imperial punishment of the cross was used against Jesus and others, a variety of methods of imperial punishment have been used against those considered to be transgressors, rebels, troublemakers, enemy combatants, or "different." The gallows, cannon, or infected blankets for indigenous Americans, the lynching rope for African Americans, the ovens for Jews, the atomic bomb for Japanese civilians, waterboarding and other kinds of torture for captured Iraqis — all of these have been justified and utilized.

The challenge for Christians today is not to participate in such violence, to learn how to welcome strangers, immigrants, and those who are "other," how to love enemies, how to break down dividing walls, how to reconcile those who are estranged, and how to convert all of our instruments of death and violence into symbols of life.

3. Crown

The UCC chose the crown as a symbol to signify "the kingship of the Risen Christ over all the world." In these days of ceremonial kings and queens, however, perhaps it would be better to let the "crown" symbolize Jesus' central vision of an earthly kingdom (empire, realm, conmonwealth, kin-dom) of God.

John Dominic Crossan defines "the Kingdom of God" as "what the world would look like if and when God sat on Caesar's throne, or if and when God lived in Antipas's palace."[2] God's kingdom is where God's will is done on earth. It is about the transformation of this world into holiness and justice. Thus it is both a political and a religious idea: to whom does the world belong, and how should it be run?

These are key questions confronting the UCC (and every church) today.

4. Comma

The members of the UCC are on a journey today. We invite others to join us as we travel into the future, listening to and seeking to be faithful to a still-speaking God.

This says something about our internal life together. As UCC biblical scholar Stephen Patterson has written, "Jesus gathered at table all sorts of people: men and women, clean and unclean, lepers and Pharisees, Jews and Gentiles, poor and rich — he gathered them all around a common table. One sees this all the time in the gospels. The open table — the symbol of unbrokered access — we still celebrate it today when the Lord's Supper is offered as an open table."[3]

And it says something about our external life — our activity in the world. As mentioned previously, we are at a very critical point in our planet's history. Desperately needed are earth residents who see our relationship with the earth and its inhabitants as one of stewardship rather than dominion, reverence rather than contempt. As Patterson has also written, "Jesus ... by his word and deed called into question the structures of his social world that dehumanized and made expendable so many precious human beings of God's own making."[4]

Desperately needed are people of faith to help mend and repair the earth and human relationships. We need the conviction that

---

2. John Dominic Crossan, *God and Empire*, 116.
3. Stephen Patterson, "Shall We Teach What Jesus Taught?" *Prism* 11, no. 1 (1996):51.
4. Stephen J. Patterson, *The God of Jesus: The Historical Jesus and the Search for Meaning* (Harrisburg, Pa.: Trinity Press International, 1998), 83.

each life is holy, to be honored, valued, and enhanced — in the United States, Iraq, or anywhere else in the world.

God is challenging the UCC today to be a church of "pros":

- *professing*: declaring by its faithfulness to Jesus' way of life the good news of God's love and justice;

- *proleptic*: living the future God intends for us as if it were already present;

- *prophetic*: speaking, by word and deed, on behalf of a still-speaking God.

The UCC is on an exciting journey. If you are not "on the road" yet, come join us!

OPEN MY EYES THAT I MIGHT HEAR

The larger vision of the biblical narrative — a vision we in the United Church of Christ aspire to — is of God's peaceable kingdom. It's a vision shared not only by cows and donkeys, lions and lambs, but by Moses, the prophets of Israel, and Jesus. All of these wait and long for the culmination of God's kingdom when the wolf shall lie down with the lamb (Isa. 11:6) and God will once again dwell in the midst of the people (Rev. 21:5).

This is a glorious vision indeed. But, sad to say, throughout the Bible God's kingdom is repeatedly thwarted both by foreign powers and by the idolatrous actions of Israel itself. Obedience to kings repeatedly takes precedence over faithfulness to the God of Israel.

It all starts when God's chosen ones — the Israelites — are summoned to freedom from the bondage and predictability of Pharaoh's Egypt. Through this story we learn that while God offers true, covenantal freedom, the powers and principalities offer a powerfully seductive — *albeit false* — sense of security.

Upon winning their freedom from Egyptian bondage, Israel moves from slavery, to a tribal confederacy, and finally to a monarchy resembling the nations around them (1 Sam. 8). The God of Israel who is free, elusive, and just is eventually shackled in the Jerusalem Temple, underwriting a royal agenda of accumulation and exploitation.

These "glory days" of Israel, developed most powerfully under King Solomon, were also the beginning of the end. Seduced by worldly idols, they fell vulnerable to Babylon. Israel would now be God's remnant community living according to the will of successive powers that inhabited it. Gone was Israel's promised land of milk and honey.

Into this historical situation of communal dislocation would come two conflicting powers: that of the Roman Empire and that of Jesus. The forces of violence and exploitation known throughout history culminated in the image of Rome's emperor Caesar. This empire, though, would be confronted by the power of justice, compassion, and love embodied in the Son of God, Jesus of Nazareth. It is into the midst of this struggle, waged again and again throughout history, that the United Church of Christ finds its call.

In the midst of the power of empire, we shall listen and act. We shall tune in to the still-speaking God.

QUOTES FOR OUR JOURNEY

"We accomplish in our lifetimes only a tiny fraction of the magnificent enterprise that is God's work.... Nothing we do is complete... but it is a beginning, a step along the way, an opportunity for God's grace to enter.... We are prophets of a future not our own."

—Oscar Romero, Archbishop of San Salvador

"Nothing worth doing is completed in our lifetime; therefore, we must be saved by hope. Nothing true or beautiful or good makes complete sense in any immediate context of history; therefore we must be saved by faith. Nothing we do, however virtuous, can be accomplished alone; therefore, we are saved by love."

—Reinhold Niebuhr, UCC theologian

"Have patience with everything unresolved in your heart and try to love the questions themselves as if they were locked rooms or books written in a very foreign language. Don't search for the answers.... Live the questions now. Perhaps then, someday far in the future, you will gradually, without even noticing it, live your way into the answer."

—Rainier Maria Rilke, Austrian poet

"Our first task in approaching another people, another culture, another religion, is to take off our shoes, for the place we are approaching is holy. Else we may find ourselves treading on [people's] dreams. More serious still, we may forget that God was here before our arrival.

"We have, then, to ask what is the authentic religious content in [their] experience. We may, if we have asked humbly and respectfully, still reach the conclusion that our brothers [and sisters] have started from a false premise and reached a faulty conclusion. But we must not arrive at our judgment from outside their religious situation.

"We have to try to sit where they sit, to enter sympathetically into the pains and griefs and joys of their history and see how those pains and griefs and joys have determined the premises of their argument. We have, in a word, to be 'present' with them."

—John V. Taylor, author, *The Primal Vision*

"For Christians, reconciliation will mean plumbing the biblical claim that this breaking down of walls of hostility and reconciling has already taken place through the Prophet of Nazareth, the Announcer of Jubilee, the Healer of Brokenness, the Breaker of Purity Codes, the Overturner of Commodity Tables, the Criminal of Golgotha, and the One who walks with us along our Emmaus roads."

— Theodore A. Braun, author,
Perspectives on Cuba and Its People

THE PHOENIX AFFIRMATIONS (Version 3.8)

The public face of Christianity in America today bears little connection to the historic faith of our ancestors. It represents even less our own faith as Christians who continue to celebrate the gifts of our Creator, revealed and embodied in the life, death, and resurrection of Jesus Christ. Heartened by our experience of the transforming presence of Christ's Holy Spirit in our world, we find ourselves in a time and place where we will be no longer silent. We hereby mark an end to our silence by making the following affirmations:

As people who are joyfully and unapologetically Christian, we pledge ourselves completely to the way of Love. We work to express our love, as Jesus teaches us, in three ways: by loving God, neighbor, and self.[5]

Christian love of God includes...

1. Walking fully in the path of Jesus, without denying the legitimacy of other paths that God may provide for humanity;

2. Listening for God's word, which comes through daily prayer and meditation, studying the ancient testimonies that we call scripture, and attending to God's present activity in the world;

---

5. See Matt. 22:34–40 (and parallels in Mark 12:28–31 and Luke 10:25–28); cf. Deut. 6:5; Lev. 19:18.

3. Celebrating the God whose Spirit pervades and whose glory is reflected in all of God's Creation, including the earth and its ecosystems, the sacred and secular, the Christian and non-Christian, the human and nonhuman;

4. Expressing our love in worship that is as sincere, vibrant, and artful as it is scriptural.

Christian love of neighbor includes...

5. Engaging people authentically, as Jesus did, treating all as creations made in God's very image, regardless of race, gender, sexual orientation, age, physical or mental ability, nationality, or economic class;

6. Standing, as Jesus does, with the outcast and oppressed, the denigrated and afflicted, seeking peace and justice with or without the support of others;

7. Preserving religious freedom and the church's ability to speak prophetically to government by resisting the commingling of church and state;

8. Walking humbly with God, acknowledging our own shortcomings while honestly seeking to understand and call forth the best in others, including those who consider us their enemies.

Christian love of self includes...

9. Basing our lives on the faith that in Christ all things are made new and that we, and all people, are loved beyond our wildest imagination — for eternity;

10. Claiming the sacredness of both our minds and our hearts, and recognizing that faith and science, doubt and belief serve the pursuit of truth;

11. Caring for our bodies and insisting on taking time to enjoy the benefits of prayer, reflection, worship, and recreation in addition to work;

12. Acting on the faith that we are born with a meaning and purpose, a vocation and ministry that serve to strengthen and extend God's realm of love.

POSTSCRIPT

In this handbook you will find a concise description of the United Church of Christ, its history, practices, structures, opportunities, and challenges. It is not a comprehensive description. That would mean volumes, and probably a set of wheels for each volume to make it easier to transport. We hope that you will forgive the inevitable omissions and hail those new ideas and thoughts that we surely hope we have included.

We have tried to give a brief glimpse into the reality of the United Church of Christ — a church that has struggled to be open to the Holy Spirit and to what Jesus was passionate about. Sometimes it has failed, but always it has tried to stay in the struggle — learning, changing, growing, failing, but never giving up. It is not an easy church with all the answers, but it is a resurrection church awed by the reality and responsibility of what that means. It is a church on a journey into the future. It is a comma church that believes that God is still speaking to us today.

Two New Songs

MAYBE GOD IS STILL SPEAKING*

I don't know why eagles still fly,
    rivers still run to the sea,
I don't know why babies still cry,
    and people still long to be free.
I don't know why seasons go by,
    planets and galaxies twirl;
Maybe God is still speaking
    with the voice of a turning world.

I don't know why flowers appear,
    born of the sun and the rain;
I don't know why snowflakes appear
    with no two exactly the same;
I don't know why earth is the home
    to so many colors and kinds;
Maybe God is still speaking
    on the faces of humankind.

Maybe God is still speaking,
    speaking to us today!
Maybe God is still speaking,
    what if God still has something to say?

I don't know why some people die,
    others continue to live;

I don't know why some have so much,
    while others have nothing to give.
I don't know why some people laugh,
    others have eyes full of tears;
Maybe God is still speaking,
    in the language of hopes and fears!

Maybe God is still speaking,
    speaking to us today!
Maybe God is still speaking,
    what if God still has something to say?

Open our ears, open our eyes,
    speak through the wind and the storm,
Lighten our hearts, light up our souls,
    help us endure till the morn.
Speak what is true, old words and new,
    say You've been here all the while!
Maybe God is still speaking,
    with the voice of a little child,
    the voice of an infant.

Soften our hearts, strengthen our will,
    save us from closing our minds!
Open our hearts and minds!
Maybe God is still speaking,
    Still speaking to humankind!
Maybe God is still speaking to us today,
    God still has something to say,
Speaking to us today!

CALLED TO MINISTRY*

Tune: CWM Rhondda

God, you call us to your service,
    call to claim our ministry.
You have given Christ as servant,
    helping us serve faithfully.
We respond then, each uniquely —
    we are all in ministry.
We are all in ministry.

You call us to share the good news,
    share with love so joyfully
that all people may have blessings,
    may live life so full and free.
That's the good news. Shout the good news!
We are your evangelists.
We are your evangelists.

God you ask us to take care of
    all created by your hand —
care for planet, birds and flowers,
    all your people, every land.
We are striving to be careful,
We are stewards of your gifts.
We are stewards of your gifts.

---

*Words: Earl D. Miller. From Marin Tirabassi and Maria Tirabassi, eds., *Before the Amen: Creative Resources for Worship,* 193–94. This was written by Earl D. Miller on the occasion of the Ordination of Lori Miller Lewis. The second to the last stanza in the original, which focuses on this ordination event, is given here:

    Now we call upon your Spirit, Holy Spirit, come and claim
    This your servant, gifted, faithful, this your child whom we ordain.
    We lay hands and feel your power, power for special ministry.
    For your gifts of ministry.

Taught by Christ, we all are teachers,
reaching out to young and old.
Let us nurture truth and justice
molded by the faith we hold.
We are teachers, we are learners,
growing through your loving Word,
Growing through your loving Word.

Christ calls us to serve God's people.
We each have our ministry.
As we labor, as we worship,
we seek global harmony.
God we praise you, God, we thank you,
for your gifts of ministry.
For your gifts of ministry.

More Resources

A CHAPTER A DAY KEEPS THE EMPIRE AWAY
(or, Nourishment for the Journey
from High-Nutrient Books)

History of the UCC

Bailey, J. Martin, and W. Evan Golder. *UCC @ 50: Our History, Our Future* (UCC Resources, 700 Prospect Avenue, Cleveland, OH 44115-1100).

Zikmund, Barbara Brown, series ed. *The Living Theological Heritage of the United Church of Christ.* Cleveland: Pilgrim Press.

    Vol. 1: *Ancient and Medieval Legacies* (1995).

    Vol. 2: *Reformation Roots* (1997).

    Vol. 3: *Colonial and National Beginnings* (1998).

    Vol. 4: *Consolidation and Expansion* (1999).

    Vol. 5: *Outreach and Diversity* (2000).

    Vol. 6: *Growing Toward Unity* (2001).

    Vol. 7: *United and Uniting* (2005).

Our biblical grounding

Borg, Marcus J. *Jesus: Uncovering the Life, Teachings, and Relevance of a Religious Revolutionary.* New York: HarperOne, 2008.

———. *Reading the Bible Again for the First Time: Taking the Bible Seriously but Not Literally.* New York: HarperSanFrancisco, 2002.

Borg, Marcus J., and John Dominic Crossan. *The First Christmas: What the Gospels Really Teach About Jesus' Birth.* New York: HarperOne, 2007.

———. *The Last Week. A Day-by Day Account of Jesus's Final Week in Jerusalem.* San Francisco: HarperSanFrancisco, 2006.

Brueggemann, Walter. *Biblical Perspectives on Evangelism: Living in a Three-Storied Universe.* Louisville: Westminster John Knox Press, 2003.

———. *An Introduction to the Old Testament: The Canon and Christian Imagination.* Nashville: Abingdon Press, 1993.

———. *The Prophetic Imagination.* 2nd ed. Minneapolis: Fortress Press, 2001.

Cone, James. *A Black Theology of Liberation.* Maryknoll, N.Y.: Orbis Books, 1990.

Crossan, John Dominic. *God and Empire: Jesus against Rome, Then, and Now.* San Francisco: HarperSanFrancisco, 2007.

Gomes, Peter J. *The Scandalous Gospel of Jesus: What's So Good about the Good News?* New York: HarperOne, 2007.

Gottwald, Norman K., ed. *The Bible and Liberation: Political and Social Hermeneutics.* Maryknoll, N.Y.: Orbis Books, 1983.

Gutiérrez, Gustavo. *A Theology of Liberation.* Maryknoll, N.Y.: Orbis Books, 1983.

Fiorenza, Elisabeth Schüssler, ed. *Searching the Scriptures: A Feminist Commentary.* New York: Crossroad, 1994.

Harrelson, Walter J., gen. ed. *The New Interpreter's Study Bible.* New Revised Standard Version with the Apocrypha. Nashville: Abingdon Press, 2003.

Herzog, William R., II. *Jesus, Justice, and the Reign of God: A Ministry of Liberation.* Louisville: Westminster John Knox Press, 2000.

Horsley, Richard A., ed. *Paul and Empire: Religion and Power in Roman Imperial Society.* Valley Forge, Pa.: Trinity Press International,1997.

Kolbell, Erik. *What Jesus Meant: The Beatitudes and a Meaningful Life.* Louisville: Westminster John Knox Press, 2003.

Mollenkott, Virginia Ramey. *Sensuous Spirituality: Out from Fundamentalism.* Cleveland: Pilgrim Press, 1982, 2008.

Newsome, Carol A., and Sharon H. Ringe, eds. *The Women's Bible Commentary.* Louisville: Westminster John Knox Press, 2006.

Patterson, Stephen J. *Beyond the Passion: Rethinking the Death and Life of Jesus.* Valley Forge, Pa.: Trinity Press International, 1998.

————. *The God of Jesus: The Historical Jesus and the Search for Meaning.* Minneapolis: Augsburg Fortress, 2004.

Rossing, Barbara R. *The Rapture Exposed: The Message of Hope in the Book of Revelation.* New York: Basic Books, 2004.

Spong, John Shelby. *Rescuing the Bible from Fundamentalism: A Bishop Rethinks the Meaning of Scripture.* New York: HarperOne, 1992.

————. *The Sins of Scripture: Exposing the Bible's Texts of Hate to Reveal the God of Love.* San Francisco: Harper San Francisco, 2005.

Tamez, Elsa. *The Scandalous Message of James: Faith without Works Is Dead.* New York: Crossroad, 1992.

Trible, Phyllis. *God and the Rhetoric of Sexuality.* Minneapolis: Fortress Press, 1978.

————. *Texts of Terror: Literary and Feminist Readings of the Biblical Narratives.* Minneapolis: Fortress Press,1984.

Our current situation

Bader-Saye, Scott. *Following Jesus in a Culture of Fear: Christian Practice of Everyday Life.* Grand Rapids: Brazos Press, 2007.

Culver, Sheldon, and John Dorhauer. *Steeplejacking: How the Christian Right Is Hijacking Mainstream Religion.* Brooklyn, N.Y.: Ig Publishing, 2007.

Dorrien, Gary. *Imperial Designs: Neoconservatism and the New Pax Americana.* New York: Routledge, 2004.

Ellison, Marvin M., and Judith Plaskow, eds. *Heterosexism in Contemporary World Religion: Problem and Prospect.* Cleveland: Pilgrim Press, 2007.

Lynn, Barry W. *Piety and Politics: The Right-Wing Assault on Religious Freedom.* New York: Random House Harmony Books, 2006.

Maguire, Daniel C. *A Moral Creed for All Christians.* Minneapolis: Fortress Press, 2005.

Maguire, Daniel C., and Sa'diyya Shaikh, eds. *Violence against Women in Contemporary World Religion: Roots and Cures.* Cleveland: Pilgrim Press, 2007.

Meyers, Robin. *Why the Christian Right Is Wrong: A Minister's Manifesto for Taking Back Your Faith, Your Flag, Your Future.* Los Angeles: Jossey-Bass, 2006.

Raushenbush, Paul, ed. *Christianity and the Social Crisis in the 21st Century: The Classic That Woke Up the Church.* Featuring Walter Rauschenbusch. New York: HarperOne, 2007.

Ruether, Rosemary Radford, and Rosemary Skinner Keller, eds. *In Our Own Voices: Four Centuries of American Women's Religious Writing.* San Francisco: HarperSanFrancisco, 1995.

Wink, Walter, ed. *Homosexuality and the Christian Faith: Questions of Conscience for the Churches.* Minneapolis: Fortress Press, 1999.

Moving into the future

Elnes, Eric. *The Phoenix Affirmations: A New Vision for the Future of Christianity.* Los Angeles: Jossey-Bass, 2006.

Dorrien, Gary J. *Reconstructing the Common Good: Theology and the Social Order.* Maryknoll, N.Y.: Orbis Books, 1990.

Schwartzentruber, Michael, ed. *The Emerging Christian Way: Thoughts, Stories, and Wisdom for a Faith of Transformation.* Kelowna, B.C.: CopperHouse, 2006.

Tirabassi, Marin, and Maria Tirabassi, eds. *Before the Amen: Creative Resources for Worship.* Cleveland: Pilgrim Press, 2007.

PERIOD-ICALS FOR COMMA READERS

United Church of Christ

United Church News, bimonthly publication of the UCC (700 Prospect Avenue, Cleveland, OH 44115-1100).

Other religious publications

The Christian Century, a biweekly magazine with the tag line "Thinking Critically, Living Faithfully" focusing on ecumenical church issues (104 S. Michigan Avenue, Suite 700, Chicago, IL 60603-5901).

National Catholic Reporter, an independent newsweekly "seeking to inform and inspire a just and peaceful world, serving as a platform for discussion of church, society and global community" (P.O. Box 41009, Kansas City, MO 64141-1109).

The Progressive Christian (formerly *Zion's Herald*), a bimonthly magazine focusing on "Faith and the Common Good" (P.O. Box 458, North Berwick, ME 03906).

Sojourners, a monthly magazine "addressing issues of faith, politics and culture from a biblical perspective" (3333 14th Street NW, Suite 200, Washington, DC 20010).

Tikkun, a bimonthly magazine focusing on politics, spirituality, and culture from a Jewish ecumenical perspective. *Tikkun* is a Hebrew word that means "to mend, repair, and transform the world" (2342 Shattuck Avenue, #1200, Berkeley, CA 94704).

Secular publications

CounterPunch, a semimonthly publication (P.O. Box 228, Petrolia, CA 95558).

The Hightower Lowdown, a monthly publication (P.O. Box 20596, New York, NY 10011).

The Progressive Populist, a semimonthly independent journal offering a wide selection of articles by progressive writers (P.O. Box 487 Storm Lake, IA 50588-0487).

The Washington Spectator, a semimonthly publication (Old Chelsea Station, P.O. Box 494, New York, NY 10113)

AND A LITTLE MOUSE SHALL LEAD THEM

Church information

www.ucc.org. The national website of the denomination.
www.churchworldservice.org. The humanitarian aid agency used by UCC.
www.godisstillspeaking.com. The God Is Still Speaking website.
www.chhsm.org. Council for Health and Human Service Ministries.
www.his.com/~mhunt/index.htm. Source for Feminist Theology.
www.religion-online.org. Source for literary materials.
www.unitedchurchpress.com. Books, resources, and church supplies.

National and world information

We in the United States live in an information bubble. Most of our news comes from newspaper and television sources controlled by large media corporations that are closely aligned with our government and reflect its official viewpoint. The websites in this last category offer articles and commentary from independent sources in our nation and around the world. They are very helpful to people of faith who want to break out of this bubble and to keep up with "the rest of the story" of what is going on in God's world.

> *www.commondreams.com*
> *www.counterpunch.org*
> *www.democracynow.org*
> *www.tomdispatch.com*
> *www.truthout.org*

HOW TO FIND A LOCAL CHURCH

There are a number of ways to locate the nearest United Church of Christ. The church page of the weekend edition of the local newspaper or the yellow pages in the telephone directory should be of help. Otherwise, the best way to find a local church is to go onto the Internet and look at *www.ucc.org*. On that webpage you will find links to find a church. It's easy. It works.

Then you have a name, address, and phone number of the church. You might even find their website. But what if that website hasn't been updated since Pharaoh was King of Egypt? It may be a sign that you have not yet found the place where you can grow.

Call the church if all else fails. Check on the time of the worship service and show up. Did people talk with you? Did you find the facility easy to understand? (Could you read the sign that said, "I John"? Maybe you didn't need the bathroom.) Did your kids feel comfortable in the nursery? Or, if the kids felt comfortable, ask them this, "Did your parents feel comfortable in worship?" (Remember, kids, parents should not be too comfortable in worship.)

What is important to you when you think about church? Music, sermons, community, outreach programs, whether or not they serve Fair Trade Coffee at Coffee Hour, whether or not the church has a bike rack, if you can wear jeans? There are many reasons why we fit or don't fit in a church. If you find one you like, can you imagine ways in which you can be involved there? Do you feel a possibility for singing in the choir or teaching Sunday School? Are there educational opportunities that you know you will want to attend? Can you imagine your family or friends attending or visiting there? What about their justice work? Are they doing things that you can support and that really address concerns you have for the world?

These are just some of the reasons people join churches. You'll have to think of what is important to you and weigh your decision. We hope you will find a UCC church near you.

Index